A gift for

....

From

....

Date

....

Calm
Moments
for
Anxious Days

A 90-Day Devotional Journey

MAX LUCADO

THOMAS NELSON
Since 1798

Contents

"Do not let your hearts be troubled."

John 14:1

Set Free

*The LORD is my light and my salvation; whom shall I fear? The
LORD is the strength of my life; of whom shall I be afraid?*
PSALM 27:1 NKJV

Fear, it seems, has taken a hundred-year lease on the building
next door and set up shop. Oversized and rude, unhealthy fear is
unwilling to share the heart with happiness. Happiness complies and
leaves. Do you ever see the two together? Can one be happy and afraid
at the same time? Clear-thinking and afraid? Confident and afraid?
Merciful and afraid? No. Fear is the big bully in the high school hall-
way: brash, loud, and unproductive. . . . Fear herds us into a prison
and slams the doors.

Wouldn't it be great to walk out?

Imagine your life wholly untouched by angst. What if faith, not
fear, was your default reaction to threats? If you could hover a fear
magnet over your heart and extract every last shaving of dread, insecurity, and doubt, what would remain? Envision a day, just one day,
absent the dread of failure, rejection, and calamity. Can you imagine a
life with no fear? This is the possibility behind Jesus' question: "Why
are you afraid?" he asks (Matthew 8:26 NCV).

A whole day without fear might seem like too big of a leap right
now. I understand that. What if you tried ten minutes? Take a deep
breath. Think about something true and lovely. Or think about
something funny. Once you've allowed yourself the gift of a fearless few minutes, go ahead and fill your mind with these promises
of God. And remember, if fear, not faith, is your default reaction,

you are not alone in that. But what if the opposite were true? With Christ, it's more than possible; it's his promise. When fear imprisons you and bullies your happiness away, remember this:

My Scripture of Hope

Surely God is my salvation; I will trust and not be afraid. The LORD, the LORD himself, is my strength and my defense; he has become my salvation.

ISAIAH 12:2

_____

_____

_____

_____

My Anxious Thoughts to Release

_____

_____

_____

God's Promise to Me

The Lord is my light and my salvation. He
will lead me out of the prison of fear.

My Prayer

_____

_____

The Lord Is with Me

You are with me; Your rod and Your staff, they comfort me.

PSALM 23:4 NKJV

Y ou are with me."

Yes, you, Lord, are in heaven. Yes, you rule the universe. Yes, you sit upon the stars and make your home in the deep. But yes, yes, yes, you are with me.

The Lord is with me. The Creator is with me. Yahweh is with me.

Moses proclaimed it: "What great nation has a god as near to them as the LORD our God is near to us" (Deuteronomy 4:7 NLT).

Paul announced it: "He is not far from any one of us" (Acts 17:27).

And David discovered it: "You are with me."

Somewhere in the pasture, wilderness, or palace, David discovered that God meant business when he said: "I will not leave you" (Genesis 28:15).

Do not assume God is watching from a distance. Choose to be the person who clutches the presence of God with both hands: "The LORD is with me; I will not be afraid. What can mere mortals do to me?" (Psalm 118:6).

When the cares of this world rush at us, it's easy to forget that the Lord is with us. We get caught up in hurries and demands. Our thoughts run away with worries, leaving us anxious and exhausted. In those moments, let's remember this:

My Scripture of Hope

"So do not fear, for I am with you; do not be dismayed, for I am your God. I will strengthen you and help you; I will uphold you with my righteous right hand."

ISAIAH 41:10

_____

_____

_____

_____

_____

_____

_____

My Anxious Thoughts to Release

_____

_____

_____

God's Promise to Me

The Lord is with me. No matter how I feel. No matter what I am facing. The Lord is with me. Always.

My Prayer

_____

_____

_____

Believe He Can

"Don't be afraid; just believe."
MARK 5:36

T he presence of fear does not mean you have no faith. Fear visits everyone. Even Christ was afraid (Mark 14:33). But make your fear a visitor and not a resident. Hasn't fear taken enough? Enough smiles? Chuckles? Restful nights, exuberant days? Meet your fears with faith.

Do what my father urged my brother and me to do. Summertime for the Lucado family always involved a trip from West Texas to the Rocky Mountains. (Think Purgatory to Paradise.) My dad loved to fish for trout on the edge of the white-water rivers. Yet he knew that the currents were dangerous and his sons could be careless. Upon arrival we'd scout out the safe places to cross the river. He'd walk us down the bank until we found a line of stable rocks. He was even known to add one or two to compensate for our short strides.

As we watched, he'd test the stones, knowing if they held him, they'd hold us. Once on the other side, he'd signal for us to follow.

"Don't be afraid," he could have said. "Trust me."

We children never needed coaxing. But we adults often do. Does a river of fear run between you and Jesus? Cross over to him.

Believe he can. Believe he cares.

Does the path ahead look uncertain, even frightening? Maybe this image will help. When a father leads his four-year-old son down a crowded street, he takes him by the hand and says, "Hold on to me." He doesn't say, "Memorize the map." Or, "Take your chances

dodging the traffic." Or, "Let's see if you can find your way home."
The good father gives the child one responsibility: "Hold on to my
hand." When fears threaten your faith, remember this:

My Scripture of Hope

You go before me and follow me. You place your hand of
blessing on my head.

PSALM 139:5 NLT

_____

_____

_____

_____

_____

My Anxious Thoughts to Release

_____

_____

_____

God's Promise to Me

I don't have to live afraid. Because God cares. He
holds my hands and leads me safely to him.

My Prayer

_____

_____

"Here Is God"

"I am with you always, even to the end of the age."
MATTHEW 28:20 NKJV

When ancient sailors sketched maps of the oceans, they disclosed their fears. On the vast unexplored waters, cartographers wrote words such as these:

"Here be dragons."

"Here be demons."

"Here be sirens."

Were a map drawn of your world, would we read such phrases? Over the unknown waters of adulthood, "Here be dragons." Near the sea of the empty nest, "Here be demons." Next to the farthermost latitudes of death and eternity, do we read, "Here be sirens"?

If so, take heart from the example of Sir John Franklin. He was a master mariner in the days of King Henry V. Distant waters were a mystery to him, just as they were to other navigators. Unlike his colleagues, however, Sir John Franklin was a man of faith. The maps that passed through his possession bore the imprimatur of trust. On them he had crossed out the phrases "Here be dragons," "Here be demons," "Here be sirens." In their place he wrote the phrase "Here is God."

Mark it down. You will never go where God is not. You may be transferred, enlisted, commissioned, reassigned, or hospitalized, but—brand this truth on your heart—you can never go where God is not. "I am with you always," Jesus promised (Matthew 28:20).

Don't be afraid; just believe.

There are times when our travels cover the miles. And there are times when they take us on journeys through troubles and the murky places of our own hearts. When you are tempted to write "Here be dragons" over the shadowy corners of your life, instead write "Here be God" and remember this:

My Scripture of Hope

If I go up to the heavens, you are there; if I make my bed in the depths, you are there. If I rise on the wings of the dawn, if I settle on the far side of the sea, even there your hand will guide me, your right hand will hold me fast.

PSALM 139:8–10

_____

_____

_____

My Anxious Thoughts to Release

_____

_____

God's Promise to Me

I can never go where God is not. He is with
me always. And he holds fast to me.

My Prayer

_____

_____

God Is Righteous

He is gracious, and full of compassion, and righteous.
PSALM 112:4 NKJV

Righteousness is who God is. God's righteousness "endures forever" (Psalm 112:3) and "reaches to the skies" (Psalm 71:19 NCV).

God is righteous. His decrees are righteous (Romans 1:32). His judgment is righteous (Romans 2:5). His requirements are righteous (Romans 8:4). His acts are righteous (Daniel 9:16). Daniel declared, "Our God is righteous in everything he does" (Daniel 9:14).

God is never wrong. He has never rendered a wrong decision, experienced the wrong attitude, taken the wrong path, said the wrong thing, or acted the wrong way. He is never too late or too early, too loud or too soft, too fast or too slow. He has always been and always will be right. He is righteous.

God is perfectly righteous, *and* he has complete sovereignty over his creation. *Sovereignty* is how the Bible describes God's perfect control and management of the universe. He preserves and governs every element. He is continually involved with all created things, especially the lives of his beloved children.

Anxiety is often the consequence of perceived chaos. If we sense we are victims of unseen, turbulent, random forces, we are troubled. But his righteousness, combined with his sovereignty, add up to this fact: we can trust him, his decisions, and his ability to see us through our fears. If the chaos of this world causes you to forget that, remember this:

My Scripture of Hope

Those who know your name trust in you, for you, LORD, have never forsaken those who seek you.

PSALM 9:10

_____

_____

_____

_____

_____

_____

_____

_____

_____

My Anxious Thoughts to Release

_____

_____

_____

God's Promise to Me

Because God is righteous, I can trust his decisions. Because he is sovereign, I can trust his power. I can trust God.

My Prayer

_____

_____

An Awareness of God

Devote yourselves to prayer, being watchful and thankful.

Colossians 4:2

E arly Christians were urged to

- "pray without ceasing" (1 Thessalonians 5:17 nasb);
- "never stop praying" (Romans 12:12 cev);
- "pray in the Spirit at all times and on every occasion" (Ephesians 6:18 nlt).

Sound burdensome? Are you wondering, *My business needs attention, my children need dinner, my bills need paying. How can I stay in a place of prayer?*

Do this. Change your definition of prayer. Think of prayer less as an activity for God and more as an awareness of God. Seek to live in uninterrupted awareness. Acknowledge his presence everywhere you go. As you stand in line to register your car, think, *Thank you, Lord, for being here.* In the grocery as you shop, *Your presence, my King, I welcome.* As you wash the dishes, worship your Maker.

God loves the sound of your voice. Always. He doesn't hide when you call. He hears your prayers. For that reason, "Be anxious for nothing, but in everything by prayer and supplication, with thanksgiving, let your requests be made known to God" (Philippians 4:6 nkjv).

Sometimes we look at prayer as an item on our to-do list instead of a lifeline to love and connection. We think prayer has to be in quiet places, in reverent frames of mind, with holy words. But what if "praying without ceasing" is an awareness of God and his gifts? A path to peace that blunts the worries of this world? If you have a checklist for prayer that is limiting your conversations with God, remember this:

My Scripture of Hope

We do not know how to pray as we should. But the Spirit himself speaks to God for us, even begs God for us with deep feelings that words cannot explain.

ROMANS 8:26 NCV

My Anxious Thoughts to Release

God's Promise to Me

God hears me *always*. Even over the noise of life.
Even when I don't use words to speak.

My Prayer

He Rescues

Not to us, Lord . . . but to Your name give glory,
because of Your mercy, because of Your truth.
Psalm 115:1 nasb

G od has one goal: God. "I have my reputation to keep up" (Isaiah 48:11 msg).

Surprised? Isn't such an attitude, dare we ask, self-centered? Don't we deem this behavior "self-promotion"? Why does God broadcast himself?

For the same reason the pilot of the lifeboat does. Think of it this way. You're floundering neck-deep in a dark, cold sea. Ship sinking. Life jacket deflating. Strength waning. Through the inky night comes the voice of a lifeboat pilot. But you cannot see him. What do you want the driver of the lifeboat to do?

Be quiet? Say nothing? Stealth his way through the drowning passengers? By no means! You need volume! In biblical jargon, you want him to show his glory. You need to hear him say, "I am here. I am strong. I have room for you. I can save you!"

Don't we want God to do the same? Look around. People thrash about in seas of guilt, anger, despair. Life isn't working. We are going down fast. But God can rescue us. And only one message matters. His! We need to see God's glory.

We need someone to reach through the fog and save us. When we're in over our head, we need someone to reach down and pull us to safety. That someone—that *Someone*—is God. When you need a rescuer, remember this:

My Scripture of Hope

He reached down from on high and took hold of me; he drew
me out of deep waters.

PSALM 18:16

_____
_____
_____
_____
_____
_____
_____
_____
_____

My Anxious Thoughts to Release

_____
_____
_____

God's Promise to Me

God is here. He is strong. He has room for me
in his eternal lifeboat. He can save me.

My Prayer

_____
_____

Fill Your Day with G-O-D

"If any of you want to be my followers, you must forget about yourself. You must take up your cross every day and follow me."
Luke 9:23 cev

My friend and I went on an extended hill-country bike trek. A few minutes into the trip, I began to tire. Within a half hour, my thighs ached and my lungs heaved like a beached whale. I could scarcely pump the pedals. After forty-five minutes, I had to dismount to catch my breath. That's when my partner spotted the problem. Both rear brakes were rubbing my back tire! Rubber grips contested every pedal stroke. The ride was destined to be a tough one.

Don't we do the same? Guilt presses on one side. Dread drags the other. No wonder we weary so. We sabotage our day, wiring it for disasters, lugging along yesterday's troubles, downloading tomorrow's struggles. We aren't giving the day a chance.

What can we do? Here's my proposal: consult Jesus. The Ancient of Days has something to say about our days.

Saturate your day in his grace. "I tell you in solemn truth," replied Jesus, "that this very day you shall be with me in Paradise" (Luke 23:43 wnt).

Entrust your day to his oversight. "Give us each day our daily bread" (Luke 11:3).

Accept his direction. "If any of you want to be my followers, you must forget about yourself. You must take up your cross every day and follow me" (Luke 9:23 cev).

Grace. Oversight. Direction. G-O-D.

Fill your day with God. Give the day a chance.

What's holding you back today? Maybe it's a resistance you are aware of. Or, like my rear brakes, maybe it's something draining your energy that you've not yet identified. When it feels like you're barely making it up the hill or through the day, remember this:

My Scripture of Hope

What then shall we say to these things? If God is for us, who can be against us?

ROMANS 8:31 NKJV

My Anxious Thoughts to Release

God's Promise to Me

I can consult Jesus. I can saturate my day in his grace. I can entrust my day to his oversight. I can accept his direction.

My Prayer

Turn to the Father

"Father, if you are willing, take away this cup of suffering."
LUKE 22:42 NCV

Jesus was more than anxious; he was afraid.

How remarkable that Jesus felt such fear. But how kind that he told us about it. We tend to do the opposite. Gloss over our fears. Cover them up. Keep our sweaty palms in our pockets, our nausea and dry mouths a secret. Not so with Jesus. We see no mask of strength. But we do hear a request for strength.

"Father, if you are willing, take away this cup of suffering." The first one to hear his fear was his Father. He could have gone to his mother. He could have confided in his disciples. He could have assembled a prayer meeting. All would have been appropriate, but none were his priority. He went first to his Father.

Jesus went first to his Father. Oh, how we tend to go everywhere else. First to the bar, to the counselor, to the self-help book, or the friend next door. Not Jesus. The first one to hear his fear was his Father in heaven. He modeled the words of Psalm 56:3: "When I am afraid, I will put my trust in you" (NLT).

Do the same with yours. Don't avoid life's Gardens of Gethsemane. Enter them. Just don't enter them alone.

Who—or what—do we turn to first when we're suffering? When we're hurting? When anxiety takes hold? We know God is the answer. So why are we tempted to turn to the quick fix, to other people, and to the things that won't last? When you're searching for someone to turn to with your fears, remember this:

My Scripture of Hope

The name of the LORD is a strong tower; the righteous run to it and are safe.

PROVERBS 18:10 NKJV

_____
_____
_____
_____
_____
_____
_____
_____
_____
_____

My Anxious Thoughts to Release

_____
_____
_____

God's Promise to Me

I can always turn to God. He will listen to my fears. He will know just what to do. And he will lend me his strength to do it.

My Prayer

_____
_____

He's Writing Your Story

"God will help you deal with whatever hard
things come up when the time comes."
MATTHEW 6:34 MSG

You look at tomorrow's demands, next week's bills, next month's silent calendar. Your future looks as barren as the Sinai Desert. "How can I face my future?"

God knows what you need and where you'll be. Trust him. "Give your entire attention to what God is doing right now, and don't get worked up about what may or may not happen tomorrow. God will help you deal with whatever hard things come up when the time comes" (Matthew 6:34 MSG).

The Greek word for *worry*, *merimnao*, stems from the verb *merizo* (divide) and *nous* (mind). Worry cleaves the mind, splitting thoughts between today and tomorrow. Today stands no chance against it. Fretting over tomorrow's problems today siphons the strength you need for now, leaving you anemic and weak.

It is not God's will that you lead a life of perpetual anxiety. It is not his will that you face every day with dread and trepidation. He made you for more than a life of breath-stealing angst and mind-splitting worry. He has a new chapter for your life. And he is ready to write it.

Worries empower little problems and encourage them to cast big shadows over our lives. In the darkness, we struggle to see the light of God's faithfulness. We forget that he is writing our story. When worry tries to snatch the pen and write itself across your life, remember this:

My Scripture of Hope

The LORD directs the steps of the godly. . . . Though they stumble, they will never fall, for the LORD holds them by the hand.

PSALM 37:23–24 NLT

_____

_____

_____

_____

_____

_____

_____

_____

_____

My Anxious Thoughts to Release

_____

_____

_____

God's Promise to Me

God knows what I need. He is writing my
story. And he will take care of me.

My Prayer

_____

_____

The Prayers He Answers

"If you believe, you will get anything you ask for in prayer."
MATTHEW 21:22 NCV

I f you believe, you will get anything you ask for in prayer." Don't reduce this grand statement to the category of new cars and paychecks. Don't limit the promise of this passage to the selfish pool of perks and favors. The fruit God assures is far greater than earthly wealth. His dreams are much greater than promotions and proposals.

God wants you to fly. He wants you to fly free of yesterday's guilt. He wants you to fly free of today's fears. He wants you to fly free of tomorrow's grave. Sin, fear, and death. These are the mountains he has moved. These are the prayers he will answer. That is the fruit he will grant. This is what he longs to do.

Here's what I think: our biggest fears are sprained ankles to God. Here's what else I think: a lot of people live with unnecessary anxiety over temporary limps.

Let's not limit our prayers to the things of this world. Instead, let's reach out with open hearts and open hands to ask for true treasures: a freedom from worry and fear, a greater trust in him, and a peace that far exceeds our understanding. Let's dare to ask and to believe he will answer. Instead of allowing fear to hold you back and limit your prayers, remember this:

My Scripture of Hope

"I tell you the truth, if your faith is as big as a mustard seed,
you can say to this mountain, 'Move from here to there,' and
it will move. All things will be possible for you."

MATTHEW 17:20–21 NCV

_____

_____

_____

_____

_____

_____

_____

My Anxious Thoughts to Release

_____

_____

_____

God's Promise to Me

God moves mountains, so he can remove my worries
and make a way through my fears. He will answer
my prayers. He will set me free to fly.

My Prayer

_____

_____

God Sees What We Can't

No one is like the LORD our God, who rules from heaven.

PSALM 113:5 NCV

O n a trip to the United Kingdom, our family visited a castle. In the center of the garden sat a maze. Row after row of shoulder-high hedges, leading to one dead end after another. Successfully navigate the labyrinth, and discover the door to a tall tower in the center of the garden. Were you to look at our family pictures of the trip, you'd see four of our five family members standing on the top of the tower. Hmmm, someone is still on the ground. Guess who? I was stuck in the foliage. I just couldn't figure out which way to go.

Ah, but then I heard a voice from above. "Hey, Dad." I looked up to see Sara, peering through the turret at the top. "You're going the wrong way," she explained. "Back up and turn right."

Do you think I trusted her? I didn't have to. But do you know what I did? I listened. Her vantage point was better than mine. She was above the maze. She could see what I couldn't.

Don't you think we should do the same with God?

Hang in there. Trust his Word. Just like me in the maze, you need a voice to lead you out. Thank God you have One who will.

Life can be a maze of obstacles and dead ends. The fear of a wrong turn—or blocked escape—can paralyze us, send us crashing into walls, or have us running backward in retreat. We need Someone above the maze, a voice to lead us through. We need God. If you need a reminder to look up for the way out, remember this:

My Scripture of Hope

Show me the right path, O LORD; point out the road for me
to follow. Lead me by your truth and teach me, for you are
the God who saves me. All day long I put my hope in you.

PSALM 25:4–5 NLT

_____
_____
_____
_____
_____
_____
_____
_____
_____
_____

My Anxious Thoughts to Release

_____
_____

God's Promise to Me

God sees what I cannot see. He knows the perfect path for me.
I can trust him to lead me, step by step, through life's maze.

My Prayer

_____
_____

Defined by Grace

God, who is rich in mercy, because of His great love with
which He loved us . . . raised us up together . . . that . . .
He might show the exceeding riches of His grace.

Ephesians 2:4–7 nkjv

Grace defines you. As grace sinks in, earthly labels fade. Society labels you like a can on an assembly line. Stupid. Unproductive. Slow learner. Fast talker. Quitter. Cheapskate. But as grace infiltrates, criticism disintegrates. You know you aren't who they say you are. You are who God says you are. Spiritually alive. Heavenly positioned. Connected to the Father. A billboard of mercy. An honored child.

Of course, not all labels are negative. Some people regard you as handsome, clever, successful, or efficient. But even a White House office doesn't compare with being "seated . . . with him in the heavenly realms" (Ephesians 2:6 nlt).

Marinate your soul in that verse. Next time the arid desert winds blow, defining you by yesterday's struggles, reach for God's goblet of grace and drink. Grace defines who you are. People hold no clout. Only God does. According to him, you are his. Period.

What names has the world called you? What labels has it given you? Whether they're good or bad, don't listen. Because this world isn't known for telling the truth—and definitely not the whole truth. If society has you worried about who you really are, remember this:

My Scripture of Hope

Now this is what the LORD says. He created you, people of Jacob; he formed you, people of Israel. He says, "Don't be afraid, because I have saved you. I have called you by name, and you are mine."

ISAIAH 43:1 NCV

_____
_____
_____
_____
_____
_____
_____

My Anxious Thoughts to Release

_____
_____
_____

God's Promise to Me

I am not who the world says I am. I am
who God says I am. I am his.

My Prayer

_____
_____

One Step at a Time

Your word is like a lamp for my feet and a light for my path.
PSALM 119:105 NCV

Arthur Hays Sulzberger was the publisher of *The New York Times* during the Second World War. Because of the world conflict, he found it almost impossible to sleep. He was never able to banish worries from his mind until he adopted as his motto these five words—"One step enough for me"—taken from the hymn "Lead, Kindly Light."

God isn't going to let you see the distant scene either. So you might as well quit looking for it. He promises a lamp unto our feet, not a crystal ball into the future. We do not need to know what will happen tomorrow. We only need to know he leads us and "we will find grace to help us when we need it" (Hebrews 4:16 NLT).

God is leading you. Leave tomorrow's problems until tomorrow.

Oh, how we like to know the details—where we're going, which path we'll take, when we'll get there, and exactly what "there" is. In other words, we want to know what is only known by God: the future.

The next time you fear the future, rejoice in the Lord's sovereignty. Rejoice in what he has accomplished. Rejoice that he is able to do what you cannot do. Fill your mind with thoughts of God, and remember this:

My Scripture of Hope

The LORD says, "I will guide you along the best pathway for
your life. I will advise you and watch over you."

PSALM 32:8 NLT

_____

_____

_____

_____

_____

_____

_____

_____

_____

My Anxious Thoughts to Release

_____

_____

_____

God's Promise to Me

God is Lord of all times and places and things. His Word is absolute
truth. I can trust and follow him because he knows the way.

My Prayer

_____

_____

You Are Mine

Our lives are in the True One and in his Son, Jesus Christ.

1 JOHN 5:20 NCV

God knows your entire story, from first word to final breath, and with clear assessment declares, "You are mine."

My publisher made a similar decision with this book. Before agreeing to publish it, they read it—every single word. Multiple sets of editorial eyes scoured the manuscript, moaning at my bad jokes, grading my word crafting, suggesting a tune-up here and a tone-down there. We volleyed pages back and forth, writer to editor to writer, until finally we all agreed—this is it. It's time to publish or pass. The publisher could pass, mind you. Sometimes they do. But in this case, obviously they didn't. With perfect knowledge of this imperfect product, they signed on. What you read may surprise you, but not them.

What you do may stun you, but not God. With perfect knowledge of your imperfect life, God signed on.

Trust God's love. His perfect love. Don't fear that he will discover your past. He already has. Don't fear disappointing him in the future. With perfect knowledge of the past and perfect vision of the future, he loves you perfectly.

How often we put on a front for the rest of the world. Hiding our imperfections and praying no one will discover the truth. It's a lonely and fearful way to be. So we reach for acceptance, connection. We search for love in people, places, and all the wrong things when, in fact, there's only one place we'll find it: God. When you're on the hunt for perfect love, remember this:

My Scripture of Hope

God demonstrates his own love for us in this: While we were
still sinners, Christ died for us.

ROMANS 5:8

_____
_____
_____
_____
_____
_____
_____
_____
_____

My Anxious Thoughts to Release

_____
_____
_____

God's Promise to Me

With perfect knowledge of all my imperfections,
God loves me perfectly. My mistakes do not stun
him. His grace still reaches out and saves me.

My Prayer

_____
_____

We Hide, He Seeks

You were all clothed with Christ.

GALATIANS 3:27 NCV

We eat our share of forbidden fruit. We say what we shouldn't say. Go where we shouldn't go. Pluck fruit from trees we shouldn't touch.

And when we do, the shame tumbles in. And we hide. We sew fig leaves. We cover ourselves in good works and good deeds, but one gust of the wind of truth, and we are naked in our own failure.

So what does God do? Exactly what he did for our parents in the garden. He sheds innocent blood. He offers the life of his Son. And from the scene of the sacrifice, the Father takes a robe—the robe of righteousness. And does he throw it in our direction and tell us to shape up? No, he dresses us himself. He dresses us with himself. "You were all baptized into Christ, and so you were all clothed with Christ" (Galatians 3:26–27 NCV).

We hide. He seeks. We bring sin. He brings a sacrifice. We try fig leaves. He brings the robe of righteousness.

Rejoice in the Lord's mercy. Trust in his ability to forgive. No more hiding behind fig leaves. Cast yourself upon the grace of Christ and Christ alone. The saint dwells in grace, not guilt. This is the tranquil soul.

One look at the wardrobe of our past mistakes confirms that we all fall short. We may try to hide it, then worry we'll be found out. The knot in our belly cinches up just a little tighter. When the fig leaves aren't working and you're anxious for his grace, remember this:

My Scripture of Hope

I am overwhelmed with joy in the LORD my God! For he has dressed me with the clothing of salvation and draped me in a robe of righteousness.

ISAIAH 61:10 NLT

My Anxious Thoughts to Release

God's Promise to Me

I am sought after by God. His robe of righteousness covers me. His grace erases my guilt. And I can live in his peace.

My Prayer

God Meets Daily Needs

*Oh, how great is Your goodness, which You have laid up for those
who fear You, which You have prepared for those who trust in You.*

Psalm 31:19 NKJV

G ive us day by day our daily bread" (Luke 11:3 NKJV). This simple
sentence unveils God's provision plan: *live one day at a time*. God
disclosed the strategy to the Israelites in the wilderness: "I'm going to
rain down food from heaven for you. Each day the people can go out
and pick up as much food as they need for that day'" (Exodus 16:4 NLT).

Note the details of God's provision plan.

He meets daily needs daily. Quail covered the compound in the
evenings; manna glistened like fine frost in the mornings. Meat for
dinner. Bread for breakfast. The food fell every day. Not annually,
monthly, or hourly, but daily. And there is more.

He meets daily needs miraculously. When the people first saw the
wafers on the ground, "[t]he Israelites took one look and said to one
another, *man-hu* (What is it?). They had no idea what it was" (Exodus
16:15 MSG).

God had resources they knew nothing about, solutions outside
their reality, provisions outside their possibility. They saw problems;
God saw provision.

Anxiety fades as our memory of God's goodness doesn't.

Trying to meet the big and little needs of daily life is exhausting.
Some of their heaviness comes from the endlessness. When the
daily problems of life block your view of God's provision, remember this:

My Scripture of Hope

My God will meet all your needs according to the riches of
his glory in Christ Jesus.

PHILIPPIANS 4:19

_____
_____
_____
_____
_____
_____
_____
_____
_____
_____

My Anxious Thoughts to Release

_____
_____
_____

God's Promise to Me

God is good. He has promised to provide for me. I can count on him
today and tomorrow and every day after that. One day at a time.

My Prayer

_____
_____

God Doesn't Give Up

GOD's business is putting things right.

PSALM 11:7 MSG

God never gives up.

When Joseph was dropped into a pit by his own brothers, God didn't give up.

When Moses said, "Here I am, send Aaron," God didn't give up.

When the delivered Israelites wanted Egyptian slavery instead of milk and honey, God didn't give up.

When Peter worshipped him at the supper and cursed him at the fire, he didn't give up.

And when human hands fastened the divine hands to a cross with spikes, it wasn't the soldiers who held the hands of Jesus steady. It was God who held them steady. God, who would give up his only Son before he'd give up on you.

Everyone thought the life of Jesus was over—*but God.* His Son was dead and buried, but God raised him from the dead. God took the crucifixion of Friday and turned it into the celebration of Sunday.

Can he not do a reversal for you?

When worries over past mistakes and fears of the future haunt you, when you wonder if God has heard your prayers, don't give up. You have been heard in heaven. Angelic armies have been dispatched. Reinforcements have been rallied. God promises, "I will contend with him who contends with you" (Isaiah 49:25 NKJV). Whether that contention is from external enemies or internal fears, when you are tempted to give up, remember this:

My Scripture of Hope

Surely your goodness and unfailing love will pursue me all the days of my life, and I will live in the house of the LORD forever.

PSALM 23:6 NLT

My Anxious Thoughts to Release

God's Promise to Me

I am God's own child. My worries, my fears, and my mistakes do not erase his love for me. He will not give up on me.

My Prayer

Christ Can!

I work and struggle, using Christ's great strength
that works so powerfully in me.
COLOSSIANS 1:29 NCV

God was *with* Adam and Eve, walking with them in the cool of the evening.

God was *with* Abraham, even calling the patriarch his friend.

God was *with* Moses and the children of Israel. He was *with* the apostles. Peter could touch God's beard. John could watch God sleep. Multitudes could hear his voice. God was *with* them!

But he is *in* you. He will do what you cannot. Imagine a million dollars being deposited into your checking account. To any observer you look the same, except for the goofy smile, but are you? Not at all! With God *in* you, you have a million resources that you did not have before!

Can't stop worrying? Christ can. And he lives within you.

This time, instead of starting with what you have, start with Jesus. Start with his wealth, his resources, and his strength. Before you open the ledger, open your heart. Before you count coins or count heads, count the number of times Jesus has helped you face the impossible. Before you lash out in fear, look up in faith. Take a moment. Turn to your Father for help.

Every day we face things we can't do by our own power or patience. They distract us. We forget to tap into the power of the One who lives *within* us. When you're feeling overwhelmed, overburdened, and overrun, remember this:

My Scripture of Hope

"My grace is all you need. My power works best in weakness."
So now I am glad to boast about my weaknesses, so that the
power of Christ can work through me.

2 CORINTHIANS 12:9 NLT

_____

_____

_____

_____

_____

_____

_____

_____

My Anxious Thoughts to Release

_____

_____

_____

God's Promise to Me

God lives *in* me. His power is in me. I never face anything alone. He
will work through me and enable me to do what needs to be done.

My Prayer

_____

_____

Look to Jesus

*"This is the will of Him who sent Me, that everyone who sees
the Son and believes in Him may have everlasting life."*

JOHN 6:40 NKJV

It's a simple promise: "Everyone who believes in him will have eternal life" (John 3:15 NLT).

The simplicity troubles many people. We expect a more complicated cure, a more elaborate treatment. We expect a more proactive assignment, to have to conjure up a remedy for our sin.

Others of us have written our own Bible verse: "God helps those who help themselves" (Popular Opinion 1:1). We'll fix ourselves, thank you. We'll make up for our mistakes with contributions, our guilt with busyness. We'll overcome failures with hard work. We'll find salvation the old-fashioned way: we'll earn it.

Christ, in contrast, says: "Your part is to trust. Trust me to do what you can't."

By the way, you take similar steps of trust daily, even hourly. You believe the chair will support you, so you set your weight on it. You believe water will hydrate you, so you swallow it. You trust the work of the light switch, so you flip it. You have faith the doorknob will work, so you turn it.

You regularly trust power you cannot see to do work you cannot accomplish. Jesus invites you to do the same with him.

Look to Jesus . . . and believe.

Our attempts to fix what we cannot fix can lead to frustrations, striving, and a fear of never being enough. Not enough to pay for the mistakes we've made. Not enough to earn God's love and grace. Just not enough. When we struggle to recall that faith is enough for him, let's remember this:

My Scripture of Hope

To all who believed him and accepted him, he gave the right to become children of God.

JOHN 1:12 NLT

_____

_____

_____

_____

My Anxious Thoughts to Release

_____

_____

_____

God's Promise to Me

I don't have to earn my place with God. His grace saves me. He will keep the promises he has made to me. And when I struggle, he will help me believe.

My Prayer

_____

_____

Prayer Is This Simple

In all your ways acknowledge Him, and He shall direct your paths.

PROVERBS 3:6 NKJV

My father let me climb onto his lap when he drove! He'd be arrested for doing so today. But half a century ago, no one cared. Especially on a flat-as-a-skillet West Texas oil field, where rabbits outnumber people.

I loved it. Did it matter that I couldn't see over the dash? That my feet stopped two feet shy of the brake and accelerator? That I didn't know a radio from a carburetor? By no means. I helped my dad drive his truck.

Did I fear driving into the ditch? Overturning the curve? Running the tire into a rut? By no means. Dad's hands were next to mine, his eyes keener than mine. Consequently, I was fearless! Anyone can drive a car from the lap of a father.

And anyone can pray from the same perspective.

Prayer is the practice of sitting calmly in God's lap and placing our hands on his steering wheel. He handles the speed and hard curves and ensures safe arrival. And we offer our requests; we ask God to "take this cup away" (Mark 14:36 NKJV). This cup of disease, betrayal, financial collapse, joblessness, conflict, or senility. Prayer is this simple.

Jesus faced his ultimate fear with honest prayer. And we can too.

We complicate prayer, creating a checklist of proper words, places, and postures to follow. As if checking all the boxes were the only way to be sure he's listening. We approach his throne with

---

uncertainty, wondering if our request is too much—if *we're* too much. If you hesitate to talk to God, remember this:

My Scripture of Hope

I love the LORD because he hears my voice and my prayer for mercy. Because he bends down to listen, I will pray as long as I have breath!

PSALM 116:1–2 NLT

_____

_____

_____

_____

_____

My Anxious Thoughts to Release

_____

_____

_____

God's Promise to Me

God loves to hear from me. I can talk to God anywhere, anytime, about anything. And he will answer me perfectly. Every time.

My Prayer

_____

_____

Near and Active

*"I am God and not a human; I am the
Holy One, and I am among you."*
HOSEA 11:9 NCV

Before you read any further, reflect on those last four words, "I am among you." Do you believe that? Do you believe God is near? He wants you to. He wants you to know he is in the midst of your world. Wherever you are as you read these words, he is present. In your car. On the plane. In your office, your bedroom, your den. He's near.

And he is more than near. He is active.

God is in the thick of things in your world. He has not taken up residence in a distant galaxy. He has not removed himself from history. He has not chosen to seclude himself on a throne in an incandescent castle.

He has drawn near. He has involved himself in the carpools, heartbreaks, and funeral homes of our day. He is as near to us on Monday as on Sunday. In the schoolroom as in the sanctuary. At the coffee break as much as the communion table.

The Lord is near! You are not alone. You may feel alone. You may think you are alone. But there is never a moment in which you face life without help. God is near.

Sometimes our responsibilities weigh on our shoulders. And it can feel as if the rest of the world is watching to see if we'll drop it all. It's not, and we won't. Because God is near. We're not alone or on our own. When worry whispers that you are, remember this:

My Scripture of Hope

"I will live in them and walk among them. I will be their
God, and they will be my people."

2 Corinthians 6:16 nlt

_____

_____

_____

_____

_____

_____

_____

_____

_____

My Anxious Thoughts to Release

_____

_____

_____

God's Promise to Me

God is near. He is working in my life. He
will carry the weight of this load.

My Prayer

_____

_____

The Path to Peace

Don't worry about anything; instead, pray about everything.
Tell God what you need, and thank him for all he has done.
PHILIPPIANS 4:6–7 NLT

W ant to worry less? Then pray more. Rather than look forward in fear, look upward in faith. This command surprises no one. Regarding prayer, the Bible never blushes. Jesus taught people that "it was necessary for them to pray consistently and never quit" (Luke 18:1 MSG). Paul told believers, "Devote yourselves to prayer with an alert mind and a thankful heart" (Colossians 4:2 NLT). James declared, "Are any of you suffering hardships? You should pray" (James 5:13 NLT).

Rather than worry about anything, "pray about everything" (Philippians 4:6 NLT). Everything? Diaper changes and dates? Business meetings and broken bathtubs? Procrastinations and prognostications? Pray about everything.

The path to peace is paved with prayer. Less consternation, more supplication. Fewer anxious thoughts, more prayer-filled thoughts. As you pray, the peace of God will guard your heart and mind. And in the end, what could be better?

Pray about everything. That's God's invitation to us. Not shyly, but boldly. How often do we take him up on his offer? Perhaps we think, *This is not worth praying about.* Or, *I can handle this on my own. I won't bother God.* And do you ever get so bogged down you *forget* to ask for help? The truth is, God wants to hear about our struggles from our own lips. If you hesitate to hand over your worries to God, remember this:

My Scripture of Hope

"Ask and it will be given to you; seek and you will find; knock
and the door will be opened to you. For everyone who asks
receives; the one who seeks finds; and to the one who knocks,
the door will be opened."

MATTHEW 7:7–8

_____

_____

_____

_____

_____

_____

_____

My Anxious Thoughts to Release

_____

_____

_____

God's Promise to Me

I can pray about anything. I can pray about everything. I can
pray any time and all the time. God wants to hear my prayers.

My Prayer

_____

_____

You Are Needed

God, who makes everything work together, will
work you into his most excellent harmonies.

PHILIPPIANS 4:9 MSG

The Unseen Conductor prompts this orchestra we call living. When gifted teachers aid struggling students and skilled managers disentangle bureaucratic knots, when dog lovers love dogs and number crunchers zero balance the account, when you and I do the most of what we do the best for the glory of God, we are "marvelously functioning parts in Christ's body" (Romans 12:5 MSG).

You play no small part, because there is no small part to be played. "All of you together are the one body of Christ, and each one of you is a separate and necessary part of it" (1 Corinthians 12:27 TLB). "Separate" and "necessary." Unique and essential. No one else has been given your lines. The Author of the human drama entrusted your part to you alone. Live your life, or it won't be lived. We need you to be you.

You need you to be you.

In a world that's caught up in the big, bold, rich, and famous, it can feel as if our contributions don't measure up. God knows that's not true. He created you to be you, and he's here to help you be the best you that you can be. If you feel unneeded, unnecessary, or less than essential, remember this:

My Scripture of Hope

"Are not two sparrows sold for a penny? Yet not one of them will fall to the ground outside your Father's care. And even the very hairs of your head are all numbered. So don't be afraid; you are worth more than many sparrows."

MATTHEW 10:29–31

_____

_____

_____

_____

_____

_____

_____

_____

My Anxious Thoughts to Release

_____

_____

_____

God's Promise to Me

God made me to be me. He will help me be the best I can be. I am both wanted and needed in his world.

My Prayer

_____

_____

When Seasons Change

To everything there is a season, a time for
every purpose under heaven.
ECCLESIASTES 3:1 NKJV

God dispenses life the way he manages his cosmos: through seasons. When it comes to the earth, we understand God's management strategy. Nature needs winter to rest and spring to awaken. We don't dash into underground shelters at the sight of spring's tree buds. Autumn colors don't prompt warning sirens. Earthly seasons don't upset us. But unexpected personal ones certainly do.

Are you on the eve of change? Do you find yourself looking into a new chapter? Is the foliage of your world showing signs of a new season? Heaven's message for you is clear: when everything else changes, God's presence never does. You journey in the company of the Holy Spirit, who "will teach you everything and will remind you of everything I have told you" (John 14:26 NLT).

So make friends with whatever's next. Embrace it. Accept it. Don't resist it. Change is not just a part of life; change is a necessary part of God's strategy. To use us to change the world, he sometimes redirects our assignments. Gideon: from farmer to general; Mary: from peasant girl to the mother of Christ; Paul: from local rabbi to world evangelist. God may call you to a new season. But he wants you to know you'll never face the future without his help.

Change is coming. That much we know. It's not knowing *when* those changes will come or what they will bring that's worrisome. When the seasons of your life are changing and you need an unchanging rock to stand on, remember this:

My Scripture of Hope

God is our refuge and strength, an ever-present help in trouble.
PSALM 46:1

_____

_____

_____

_____

_____

My Anxious Thoughts to Release

_____

_____

_____

God's Promise to Me

God's promises do not change. His presence does not change.
I'll never face a moment without him to help me.

My Prayer

_____

_____

He Calls Your Name

*"There is joy in the presence of the angels of God
when one sinner changes his heart and life."*
LUKE 15:10 NCV

O ur faith is not in religion; our faith is in God. A hardy, daring faith that believes God will do what is right, every time. And that God will do what it takes—whatever it takes—to bring his children home.

He is the shepherd in search of his lamb. His legs are scratched, his feet are sore, and his eyes are burning. He scales the cliffs and traverses the fields. He explores the caves. He cups his hands to his mouth and calls into the canyon.

And the name he calls is yours.

He is the housewife in search of the lost coin. No matter that he has nine others, he won't rest until he has found the tenth. He searches the house. He moves furniture. All other tasks can wait. Only one matters. The coin is of great value to him. He owns it. He will not stop until he finds it. The coin he seeks is you.

There is a reason the windshield is bigger than the rearview mirror. Your future matters more than your past. . . . God is ready to write a new chapter in your life. Say with Paul, "Forgetting the past and looking forward to what lies ahead, I strain to reach the end of the race and receive the prize for which God is calling us" (Philippians 3:13–14 TLB).

So if you've wandered away—whether it's a step or a mile— and you're wondering what God will do, remember this:

My Scripture of Hope

He tends his flock like a shepherd: He gathers the lambs in
his arms and carries them close to his heart.

ISAIAH 40:11

_____
_____
_____
_____
_____
_____
_____
_____
_____

My Anxious Thoughts to Release

_____
_____
_____

God's Promise to Me

God's grace is greater than my guilt. He seeks me and calls
me by my name. He won't stop until I am home with him.

My Prayer

_____
_____

When Tomorrow Comes

"Do not worry about tomorrow, for tomorrow will worry about
its own things. Sufficient for the day is its own trouble."
MATTHEW 6:34 NKJV

An Ironman triathlete told me the secret of his success: "You last the long race by running short ones." Don't swim 2.4 miles; just swim to the next buoy. Rather than bike 112 miles, ride 10, take a break, and bike 10 more. Never tackle more than the challenge ahead.

Didn't Jesus offer the same counsel? "So don't ever worry about tomorrow. After all, tomorrow will worry about itself. Each day has enough trouble of its own" (Matthew 6:34 GW).

Face challenges in stages. You can't control your temper forever, but you can control it for the next hour. Earning a college degree can seem impossible, but studying one semester is manageable, and logging in one good week is doable. You last the long race by running the short ones.

You don't have wisdom for tomorrow's problems. But you will tomorrow. You don't have resources for tomorrow's needs. But you will tomorrow. You don't have courage for tomorrow's challenges. But you will when tomorrow comes.

How often do we pick up tomorrow's problems and carry them around today? Even as they grow heavier and harder to shoulder, we refuse to put them down. They tear us up and drag us down and rob us of the joys hidden in today. Instead of borrowing tomorrow's worries, remember this:

My Scripture of Hope

"I have told you these things, so that in me you may have peace. In this world you will have trouble. But take heart! I have overcome the world."

JOHN 16:33

_____
_____
_____
_____
_____
_____
_____
_____
_____

My Anxious Thoughts to Release

_____
_____
_____

God's Promise to Me

God will lead me through the challenges of today. He will take care of me tomorrow. His help is always right on time.

My Prayer

_____
_____

From Prayer to Peace

His peace will guard your hearts and minds
as you live in Christ Jesus.
PHILIPPIANS 4:7 NLT

Believing prayer ushers in God's peace. Not a random, nebulous, earthly peace, but his peace. Imported from heaven. The same tranquility that marks the throne room, God offers to you.

Do you think he battles anxiety? You suppose he ever wrings his hands or asks the angels for antacids? Of course not. A problem is no more a challenge to God than a twig is to an elephant. God enjoys perfect peace because God enjoys perfect power.

And he offers his peace to you. A peace that will "guard your hearts and minds as you live in Christ Jesus." Paul employs a military metaphor here. The Philippians, living in a garrison town, were accustomed to the Roman sentries maintaining their watch. Before any enemy could get inside, he had to pass through the guards. God gives you the same offer. His supernatural peace overshadows you, guarding your heart.

God oversees your world. He monitors your life. Listen carefully and you will hear him say, "Everything is secure. You can rest now." By his power you will "be anxious for nothing" (Philippians 4:6 NKJV) and discover the "peace . . . which passes all understanding" (v. 7 RSV). God doesn't worry. He doesn't wring his hands or pace or practice deep breathing—though he understands when we sometimes do. When you find yourself in need of his peace, remember this:

My Scripture of Hope

You will keep in perfect peace all who trust in you, all whose
thoughts are fixed on you!

Isaiah 26:3 nlt

_____

_____

_____

_____

_____

_____

_____

_____

_____

_____

My Anxious Thoughts to Release

_____

_____

_____

God's Promise to Me

Because God enjoys perfect power, I can enjoy
perfect peace. He stands guard over me.

My Prayer

_____

_____

Saturated in God's Love

Where God's love is, there is no fear, because
God's perfect love drives out fear.
1 JOHN 4:18 NCV

We fear rejection, so we follow the crowd. We fear not fitting in, so we take the drugs. For fear of standing out, we wear what everyone else wears. For fear of blending in, we wear what no one else wears. For fear of sleeping alone, we sleep with anyone. For fear of not being loved, we search for love in all the wrong places.

But God flushes those fears. Those saturated in God's love don't sell out to win the love of others. They don't even sell out to win the love of God.

Do you think you need to? Do you think, *If I cuss less, pray more, drink less, study more . . . if I try harder, God will love me more?* Sniff and smell Satan's stench behind those words. We all need improvement, but we don't need to woo God's love. We change because we already have God's love. God's perfect love.

Perfect love is just that—perfect, a perfect knowledge of the past and perfect vision of the future. You cannot shock God with your actions. There will never be a day that you cause him to gasp, "Whoa, did you see what she just did?" God knows your entire story, from first words to final breath, and with clear assessment declares, "You are mine."

Rejection can be crushing. And in this world, there's plenty of it to go around, isn't there? Just the fear of it can make it hard to move forward, to take the next step, to breathe. When fear of rejection is haunting you, and you need a reminder of God's perfect love, remember this:

My Scripture of Hope

The Spirit we received does not make us slaves again to fear;
it makes us children of God. With that Spirit we cry out,
"Father."

ROMANS 8:15 NCV

_____
_____
_____
_____
_____
_____
_____
_____
_____

My Anxious Thoughts to Release

_____
_____
_____

God's Promise to Me

God will not reject me. I am his. His love
for me is perfect and without end.

My Prayer

_____
_____

Jesus Takes Our Fears Seriously

"Do not fear, little flock, for it is your Father's good pleasure to give you the kingdom."

LUKE 12:32 NKJV

Fear feels dreadful. It sucks the life out of the soul, curls us into an embryonic state, and drains us dry of contentment. When fear shapes our lives, safety becomes our god. When safety becomes our god, we worship the risk-free life. Can the safety lover do anything great? Can the risk-averse accomplish noble deeds? For God? For others? No. The fear-filled cannot love deeply. Love is risky. They cannot give to the poor. Benevolence has no guarantee of return. The fear-filled cannot dream wildly. What if their dreams sputter and fall from the sky? The worship of safety emasculates greatness. No wonder Jesus wages such a war against fear.

His most common command emerges from the "fear not" genre. The gospels list some 125 Christ-issued imperatives. Of these, twenty-one urge us to "not be afraid" or "not fear" or "have courage" or "take heart" or "be of good cheer." The second most common command, to love God and neighbor, appears on only eight occasions. If quantity is any indicator, Jesus takes our fears seriously. The one statement he made more than any other was this: don't be afraid.

Don't be afraid. So easy to say; so *not easy* to do. But our Lord never gives us a directive without the tools to carry it out. And he equips us with his presence and his strength, covering us with his protection. When fear comes tapping on the door of your heart, remember this:

My Scripture of Hope

The LORD, He is the One who goes before you. He will be with you, He will not leave you nor forsake you; do not fear nor be dismayed.

DEUTERONOMY 31:8 NKJV

_____
_____
_____
_____
_____

My Anxious Thoughts to Release

_____
_____
_____

God's Promise to Me

Jesus takes my fears seriously. His love and protection cover every detail of my life. I can trust him to watch over me.

My Prayer

_____
_____

He Knows How You Feel

For because He Himself [in His humanity] has suffered in being tempted (tested and tried), He is able [immediately] to run to the cry of (assist, relieve) those who are being tempted and tested and tried [and who therefore are being exposed to suffering].

HEBREWS 2:18 AMPC

Jesus was angry enough to purge the temple, hungry enough to eat raw grain, distraught enough to weep in public, fun-loving enough to be called a drunkard, winsome enough to attract kids, weary enough to sleep in a storm-bounced boat, poor enough to sleep on dirt and borrow a coin for a sermon illustration, radical enough to get kicked out of town, responsible enough to care for his mother, tempted enough to know the smell of Satan, and fearful enough to sweat blood.

But why? Why would heaven's finest Son endure earth's toughest pain? So you would know that "He is able . . . to run to the cry of . . . those who are being tempted and tested and tried."

Whatever you are facing, he knows how you feel.

When you turn to him *for* help, he runs to you *to* help. Why? He knows how you feel. He's been there.

We've all been there. Struggling with temptation, juggling all the emotions, and convinced no one will understand. We end up feeling isolated, trapped, and scared. And we worry, *What does Jesus think of me now?* When you're certain no one—not even he—could possibly understand, remember this:

My Scripture of Hope

Our high priest is able to understand our weaknesses. He was
tempted in every way that we are, but he did not sin.

HEBREWS 4:15 NCV

_____
_____
_____
_____
_____
_____
_____
_____
_____
_____

My Anxious Thoughts to Release

_____
_____
_____

God's Promise to Me

I can go to Jesus for help. *With anything.* He will
understand. Because he's been where I've been.

My Prayer

_____
_____

See His Glory

The LORD spoke to Moses face to face, as a man speaks to his friend.
EXODUS 33:11 NKJV

Moses makes a request of God. "Show me your glory" (Exodus 33:18 NCV).

"Show me your radiance," Moses is praying. "Flex your biceps. Let me see the *S* on your chest. Your preeminence. Your heart-stopping, ground-shaking extraspectacularness."

Why did Moses want to see God's greatness?

Ask yourself a similar question. Why do you stare at sunsets and ponder the summer night sky? Why do you search for a rainbow in the mist or gaze at the Grand Canyon? How do you explain your fascination with such sights?

Beauty? Yes. But doesn't the beauty point to a beautiful Someone? Doesn't the immensity of the ocean suggest an immense Creator? Doesn't the rhythm of migrating cranes and beluga whales hint of a brilliant mind? And isn't that what we desire? A beautiful Maker? An immense Creator? A God so mighty that he can commission the birds and command the fish?

"Show me your glory, God," Moses begs.

We cross a line when we make such a request. When our deepest desire is not the things of God, or a favor from God, but God himself, we cross a threshold. Less self-focus, more God-focus. Less about me, more about him.

One glance at the skies—night or day—reveals the heart-stopping, extraspectacularness of God. His might is immeasurable and infinite. Doubt and fear would say we are nothing in the midst of such immensity and power. God says, *You are seen and you are mine.* So if you ever feel afraid of being lost in the enormity of it all, remember this:

My Scripture of Hope

When I consider your heavens, the work of your fingers, the moon and the stars, which you have set in place, what is mankind that you are mindful of them, human beings that you care for them? You have made them a little lower than the angels and crowned them with glory and honor.

Psalm 8:3–5

_____

_____

_____

My Anxious Thoughts to Release

_____

_____

_____

God's Promise to Me

God is infinite and all-powerful. He is also
personal. He sees, knows, and loves me.

My Prayer

_____

A New Day

People receive God's promise by having faith. This
happens so the promise can be a free gift.
Romans 4:16 ncv

O ur problem is not so much that God doesn't give us what we hope for as it is that we don't know the right thing for which to hope. (You may want to read that sentence again.)

Hope is not what you expect; it is what you would never dream. It is a wild, improbable tale with a pinch-me-I'm-dreaming ending. It's Abraham adjusting his bifocals so he can see not his grandson, but his son. It's Moses standing in the promised land not with Aaron or Miriam at his side, but with Elijah and the transfigured Christ.

Hope is not a granted wish or a favor performed; no, it is far greater than that. It is a zany, unpredictable dependence on a God who loves to surprise us out of our socks and be there in the flesh to see our reaction.

A new day awaits you, my friend. A new season in which you will worry less and trust more. A season with reduced fear and enhanced faith. Can you imagine a life in which you are anxious for nothing? God can. And with his help, you will experience it.

We hope for an end to our fears. We pray for the anxiety, the panic, the dread to be gone. But it whispers in the night when our guard is down. It creeps in, sneaks in, and sucks out our strength and courage. And we can start to wonder, *Is God really working in me? For me?* The answer is yes—and yes! When doubt creeps in, let's dare to keep on hoping and remember this:

My Scripture of Hope

With God's power working in us, God can do much, much
more than anything we can ask or imagine.

EPHESIANS 3:20 NCV

_____
_____
_____
_____
_____
_____
_____
_____
_____

My Anxious Thoughts to Release

_____
_____
_____

God's Promise to Me

God _is_ working in my life. He will bless me in surprising ways.
And his blessings will be greater than I could ever imagine.

My Prayer

_____
_____

You Are a Good Thing

Be kind to one another, tenderhearted, forgiving one
another, even as God in Christ forgave you.

EPHESIANS 4:32 NKJV

Our heavenly Father is kind to us. And since he is so kind to us, can't we be a little kinder to ourselves? *Oh, but you don't know me, Max. You don't know my faults and my thoughts. You don't know the gripes I grumble and the complaints I mumble.* No, I don't, but he does. He knows everything about you, yet he doesn't hold back his kindness toward you. Has he, knowing all your secrets, retracted one promise or reclaimed one gift?

No, he is kind to you. Why don't you be kind to yourself? He forgives your faults. Why don't you do the same? He believes in you enough to call you his ambassador, his follower, even his child. Why not take his cue and believe in yourself?

In his book you are a *good thing*. Be kind to yourself. God thinks you're worth his kindness. And he's a good judge of character.

God is characterized by kindness. Could we learn to extend to ourselves that same kindness? Could we replace that mental monologue with his promises? When the world is unkind and you struggle to be kind to yourself, remember this:

My Scripture of Hope

When God our Savior revealed his kindness and love, he saved us, not because of the righteous things we had done, but because of his mercy. He washed away our sins, giving us a new birth and new life through the Holy Spirit.

TITUS 3:4–5 NLT

_____
_____
_____
_____
_____
_____
_____

My Anxious Thoughts to Release

_____
_____
_____

God's Promise to Me

God never withholds his kindness from me. He
forgives me, loves me, and has a purpose for me.

My Prayer

_____
_____

The Way

Jesus answered, "I am the way and the truth and the life.
No one comes to the Father except through me."
JOHN 14:6

The story is told of a man on an African safari deep in the jungle. The guide before him had a machete and was whacking away the tall weeds and thick underbrush. The traveler, wearied and hot, asked in frustration, "Where are we? Do you know where you are taking me? Where is the path?!" The seasoned guide stopped and looked back at the man and replied, "I am the path."

We ask the same questions, don't we? We ask God, "Where are you taking me? Where is the path?" And he, like the guide, doesn't tell us. Oh, he may give us a hint or two, but that's all. If he did, would we understand? Would we comprehend our location? No, like the traveler, we are unacquainted with this jungle. So rather than give us an answer, Jesus gives us a far greater gift. He gives us himself.

Does he remove the jungle? No, the vegetation is still thick.

Does he purge the predators? No, danger still lurks.

Jesus doesn't give hope by changing the jungle; he restores hope by giving us himself. And he has promised to stay until the very end. "I am with you always, to the very end of the age" (Matthew 28:20).

We need that reminder. We all need that reminder. For when we can't see our way, we can remember that Jesus is our path.

It can be a jungle out there. And it can feel like we're whacking our way through it, not at all sure we're headed the right way. The next time you can't see the way through the weeds, remember this:

My Scripture of Hope

"This is my command—be strong and courageous! Do not be afraid or discouraged. For the LORD your God is with you wherever you go."

JOSHUA 1:9 NLT

_____
_____
_____
_____
_____
_____
_____
_____

My Anxious Thoughts to Release

_____
_____
_____

God's Promise to Me

Jesus knows the way because he is the Way. I can safely follow him. He will stay with me always.

My Prayer

_____
_____

P-E-A-C-E-F-U-L

Casting all your care upon Him, for He cares for you.
1 Peter 5:7 NKJV

Here are eight worry stoppers:

1. *Pray first.* Don't pace up and down the floors of the waiting room; pray for a successful surgery. Don't bemoan the collapse of an investment; ask God to help you.

2. *Easy now. Slow down.* Assess the problem. Take it to Jesus and state it clearly.

3. *Act on it.* The moment a concern surfaces, deal with it. Don't dwell on it.

4. *Compile a worry list.* Over a period of days, record your anxious thoughts. Then review them. How many of them turned into a reality?

5. *Evaluate your worry categories.* Your list will highlight themes of worry. Pray specifically about them.

6. *Focus on today.* God meets daily needs daily. Not weekly or annually. He will give you what you need when it is needed.

7. *Unleash a worry army.* Share your feelings with a few loved ones. Ask them to pray with and for you.

8. *Let God be enough.* Seek first the kingdom of wealth, and you'll worry over every dollar. Seek first the kingdom of health, and you'll sweat every blemish and bump. But seek first his kingdom, and you will find it. On that, you can depend.

Unleash a worry army. Let God be enough. P-E-A-C-E-F-U-L.

Worry can loom large, like a dark storm cloud over our lives. How do we capture and control such a thing? Step by step, with every step taking us nearer to our Father. When you need the strength and courage to take that first step, remember this:

My Scripture of Hope

"You will seek Me and find Me, when you search for Me with all your heart."

JEREMIAH 29:13 NKJV

My Anxious Thoughts to Release

God's Promise to Me

God is enough. If I seek him, I will find him.
And with him, I will find peace.

My Prayer

Within Reach

When Jesus had cried out again in a loud voice, he
gave up his spirit. At that moment the curtain of the
temple was torn in two from top to bottom.
MATTHEW 27:50–51

It's as if the hands of heaven had been gripping the veil, waiting for this moment. Keep in mind the size of the curtain—sixty feet tall and thirty feet wide. One instant it was whole; the next it was ripped in two from top to bottom. No delay. No hesitation.

What did the torn curtain mean? For the Jews it meant no more barrier between them and the holy of holies. No more priests to go between them and God. No more animal sacrifices to atone for their sins.

And for us? What did the torn curtain signify for us?

We are welcome to enter into God's presence—any day, any time. God has removed the barrier that separates us from him. The barrier of sin? Down. He has removed the curtain.

God welcomes you. God is not avoiding you. God is not resisting you. The curtain is down, the door is open, and God invites you in.

Peace is within reach because his presence is within reach. Why, then, do we hesitate to stretch our hand toward him? What keeps us from stepping through the curtain and into the throne room of God? Shyness? Shame? Shaking knees? Worries over our worries? Whatever it is, it isn't from him. He's inviting us in. We're welcome. When fear and hesitation create a barrier between you and God's peace, remember this:

My Scripture of Hope

Let us therefore come boldly to the throne of grace, that we
may obtain mercy and find grace to help in time of need.

HEBREWS 4:16 NKJV

My Anxious Thoughts to Release

God's Promise to Me

The barrier is gone. I am welcome in God's presence
anytime. And in his presence, I will find peace.

My Prayer

Know Your Knack

God, who makes everything work together, will
work you into his most excellent harmonies.
PHILIPPIANS 4:9 MSG

You are more than statistical chance, more than a marriage of heredity and society, more than a confluence of inherited chromosomes and childhood trauma. More than a walking weather vane whipped about by the cold winds of fate. Thanks to God, you have been "sculpted from nothing into something" (Psalm 139:15 MSG).

God never prefabs or mass-produces people. No slapdash shaping. "I make all things new," he declares (Revelation 21:5 NKJV). He didn't hand you your granddad's bag or your aunt's life; he personally and deliberately packed *you*.

You can do something no one else can do in a fashion no one else can do it. Exploring and extracting your uniqueness excites you, honors God, and expands his kingdom. So "[m]ake a careful exploration of who you are and the work you have been given, and then sink yourself into that" (Galatians 6:4 MSG).

Discover and deploy your knacks. When you do the most what you do the best, you put a smile on God's face. What could be better than that?

Each of us is personally and deliberately handcrafted by God. Our individuality is on purpose and for his purpose—and it can bring us great joy. But this world tends to value conformity over individuality. When the world minimizes, misuses, or misunderstands your gifts, when it sends you scurrying for the mass-produced mediocrity, remember this:

My Scripture of Hope

The LORD will work out his plans for my life—for your faithful love, O LORD, endures forever.

PSALM 138:8 NLT

_____
_____
_____
_____
_____
_____
_____
_____

My Anxious Thoughts to Release

_____
_____
_____

God's Promise to Me

I am God's own work. He created me unlike any other. My unique abilities are part of his design. By using them, I worship and honor him.

My Prayer

_____
_____

God's Work of Art

We are God's masterpiece.
EPHESIANS 2:10 NLT

O ver a hundred years ago, a group of fishermen were relaxing in a Scottish seaside inn. One of the men gestured widely and his arm struck the serving maid's tea tray, sending the teapot flying into the whitewashed wall. The innkeeper surveyed the damage and sighed, "The whole wall will have to be repainted."

"Perhaps not," offered a stranger. "Let me work with it."

Having nothing to lose, the proprietor consented. The man pulled pencils, brushes, and pigment out of an art box. In time, an image began to emerge: a stag with a great rack of antlers. The man inscribed his signature at the bottom, paid for his meal, and left. His name: Sir Edwin Landseer, famous painter of wildlife.

In his hands, a mistake became a masterpiece. God's hands do the same, over and over. He draws together the disjointed blotches in our life and renders them an expression of his love.

How often do we reach the end of the day and hang our head at the stack of mistakes and missed opportunities we've accumulated? How many moments do we waste worrying over them? But what if those seeming mistakes are part of masterpieces in the making? If you wonder and worry over what God must think of you, remember this:

My Scripture of Hope

"I—yes, I alone—will blot out your sins for my own sake and will never think of them again."

ISAIAH 43:25 NLT

_____

_____

_____

_____

_____

_____

_____

_____

_____

My Anxious Thoughts to Release

_____

_____

_____

God's Promise to Me

My mistakes do not lessen God's love. His forgiveness is mine for the asking. He is able to make even my mistakes part of his masterpiece.

My Prayer

_____

_____

An All-Knowing Love

Oh, the depths of the riches of the wisdom and knowledge of God!
How unsearchable his judgments, and his paths beyond tracing out!
ROMANS 11:33

God's omniscience governs his omnipotence. Infinite knowledge rules infinite strength. "He is wise in heart, and mighty in strength" (Job 9:4 KJV). "With him is wisdom and strength" (12:13 KJV).

His knowledge about you is as complete as his knowledge about the universe. "Even before a word is on my tongue, behold, O LORD, you know it altogether. . . . Your eyes saw my unformed substance; in your book were written, every one of them, the days that were formed for me, when as yet there were none of them" (Psalm 139:4, 16 ESV).

The veils that block your vision and mine do not block God's. Unspoken words are as if uttered. Unrevealed thoughts are as if proclaimed. Unoccurred moments are as if they were history. He knows the future, the past, the hidden, and the untold. Nothing is concealed from God. He is all-powerful, all-knowing, and *all-present*.

In our loneliest moments, the one who formed our inmost being and knitted us together in the womb offers us a friendship, a nearness unlike any other.

> God created our inmost and our outermost beings. He knows us better than anyone else. His love isn't based on incomplete information. He knows everything about our past and future. Every last detail. And with his infinite knowledge and wisdom, he loves us still. When loneliness pulls at you, remember this:

My Scripture of Hope

If any of you lacks wisdom, let him ask of God, who gives to all liberally and without reproach, and it will be given to him.

JAMES 1:5 NKJV

My Anxious Thoughts to Release

God's Promise to Me

God knows me completely. His love for me is perfect. His friendship is mine forever.

My Prayer

Words of Comfort

Let the message about Christ, in all its richness, fill your lives.
COLOSSIANS 3:16 NLT

H as any other book ever been described in this fashion: "For the word of God is alive and active" (Hebrews 4:12)?

"Alive and active." The words of the Bible have life! Nouns with pulse rates. Muscular adjectives. Verbs darting back and forth across the page. God works though these words. The Bible is to God what a surgical glove is to the surgeon. He reaches through them to touch deep within you.

Haven't you felt his touch?

In a late, lonely hour, you read the words "I will never fail you. I will never abandon you" (Hebrews 13:5 NLT). The sentences comfort like a hand on your shoulder.

When anxiety termites away at your peace, someone shares this passage: "Do not be anxious about anything, but in every situation, by prayer and petition, with thanksgiving, present your requests to God" (Philippians 4:6). The words stir a sigh from your soul.

Put them to use. "Let the message about Christ, in all its richness, fill your lives" (Colossians 3:16 NLT).

We all could use a word of comfort. God is ready to give it.

The Word is an awesome treasure. It is an endless source of guidance, instruction, and reassurance. So when our hearts are anxious and seeking comfort, let's remember this:

My Scripture of Hope

"Blessed is the one who trusts in the LORD, whose confidence is in him. They will be like a tree planted by the water that sends out its roots by the stream."

JEREMIAH 17:7–8

_____

_____

_____

_____

_____

_____

_____

_____

My Anxious Thoughts to Release

_____

_____

_____

God's Promise to Me

God's Word *is* truth. It is active and alive. It
comforts me and connects me to Christ.

My Prayer

_____

_____

The Great Giver

"Do not worry about your life. . . . Do not seek what you should
eat or what you should drink, nor have an anxious mind."

LUKE 12:22, 29 NKJV

Accumulation of wealth is a popular defense against fear. Since we fear losing our jobs, health care, or retirement benefits, we amass possessions, thinking the more we have, the safer we are.

If there were no God, stuff-trusting would be the only appropriate response to an uncertain future. But there is a God. And this God does not want his children to trust money.

Psalm 104 celebrates creation with twenty-three verses of itemized blessings: the heavens and the earth, the waters and streams and trees and birds and goats and wine and oil and bread and people and lions. God is the source of "innumerable teeming things, living things both small and great" (vv. 25 NKJV).

God is the great giver. The great provider. Absolutely generous and utterly dependable. The resounding and recurring message of Scripture is clear: God owns it all. God shares it all.

> The pressure is real. Bills to pay, loved ones to provide for, deadlines to meet. We so easily slip into thinking that it's all on us—and *that* opens the door to exhaustion, stress, stomach-knotting anxiety. The solution is almost too simple to believe: God owns it all *and* shares it all. The next time worry has you wondering how it will all work out, remember this:

My Scripture of Hope

You who belong to the LORD, fear him! Those who fear him will have everything they need. Even lions may get weak and hungry, but those who look to the LORD will have every good thing.

PSALM 34:9–10 NCV

My Anxious Thoughts to Release

God's Promise to Me

God is generous beyond measure. He has promised to provide for all my needs. He shares his riches and takes care of me.

My Prayer

Not at Home

You are like foreigners and strangers in this world.
I PETER 2:11 NCV

Your Shepherd knows that you were not made for this place. He knows you are not equipped for this place. So he has come to guide you out.

He has come to restore your soul. He is the perfect One to do so.

He has the right vision. He reminds you that "you are like foreigners and strangers in this world." And he urges you to lift your eyes from the jungle around you to the heaven above you.

He also has the right direction. He made the boldest claim in the history of man when he declared, "I am the way" (John 14:6 NCV). People wondered if the claim was accurate. He answered their questions by cutting a path through the underbrush of sin and death and escaping alive. He's the only One who ever did. And he is the only One who can help you and me do the same.

When you gave your life to him, he took responsibility for you. He guarantees your safe arrival into his port. You are his sheep; he is your Shepherd. You can have peace because you are not alone; you belong to God.

We don't fit in, do we? We're not quite in step with the rest of the world. And while the Bible declares this is a good thing, it's rarely an easy or a peaceful thing. Especially when we're so longing for acceptance and a place to belong. When you're reminded that this world isn't the place for you, remember this:

My Scripture of Hope

"The Lord will guide you always; he will satisfy your needs in a sun-scorched land and will strengthen your frame. You will be like a well-watered garden, like a spring whose waters never fail."

Isaiah 58:11

_____
_____
_____
_____
_____
_____
_____

My Anxious Thoughts to Release

_____
_____
_____

God's Promise to Me

I was not made for this place. I belong to God. There is always a place for me with him, at his table, in his family.

My Prayer

_____
_____

Simply Because You Are

I will extol You, O Lord, for You have lifted me up.
Psalm 30:1 NKJV

n God's book we are heading somewhere. We have an amazing destiny. We are being prepared to walk down the church aisle and become the bride of Jesus. We are going to live with him. Share the throne with him. Reign with him. We count. We are valuable. And what's more, our worth is built in! Our value is inborn.

You see, if there was anything that Jesus wanted everyone to understand, it was this: A person is worth something simply because he is a person. That is why he treated people like he did. Think about it. The girl caught with someone she shouldn't have been with—he forgave her. The untouchable leper who asked for cleansing—he touched him. And the blind welfare case who cluttered the roadside—he honored him. And the worn-out old windbag addicted to self-pity near the pool of Siloam—he healed him!

Listen closely. Jesus' love doesn't depend upon what you do for him. Not at all. In the eyes of the King, you have value simply because you are. You don't have to look nice or perform well. You value is inborn. Period.

Does it ever seem like so much of life hinges on what we earn, how we perform, and even how we look? The near-constant striving can lead us to fear failure and chip away at our confidence, even our confidence that we belong to him. When you need a reminder of who you are and whose you are, remember this:

My Scripture of Hope

"I know the plans I have for you," declares the Lord, "plans
to prosper you and not to harm you, plans to give you hope
and a future."

JEREMIAH 29:11

_____
_____
_____
_____
_____
_____
_____
_____

My Anxious Thoughts to Release

_____
_____
_____

God's Promise to Me

God loves me simply because I am. I am valuable to him.
And he has an amazing destiny planned for me.

My Prayer

_____
_____

Hope Is a Look Away

When I am afraid, I put my trust in you.
PSALM 56:3

How did Jesus endure the terror of the crucifixion? He went first to the Father with his fears. He modeled the words of Psalm 56:3: "When I am afraid, I put my trust in you."

Do the same with yours. Don't avoid life's Gardens of Gethsemane. Enter them. Just don't enter them alone. And while you're there, be honest. Pounding the ground is permitted. Tears are allowed. And if you sweat blood, you won't be the first. Do what Jesus did: open your heart.

And be specific. Jesus was. "Take this cup," he prayed. Give God the number of the flight. Tell him the length of the speech. Share the details of the job transfer. He has plenty of time. He also has plenty of compassion.

He doesn't think your fears are foolish or silly. He won't tell you to "buck up" or "get tough." He's been where you are. He knows how you feel.

And he knows what you need.

Don't measure the size of the mountain; talk to the One who can move it. Instead of carrying the world on your shoulders, talk to the One who has the universe on his. Hope is a look away.

It's easy to forget that Jesus was human once. We get caught up in his miracles and divinity—and those are so important to remember—but we forget that our Lord understands all we face because he once faced it too. He's been where we now stand. Walked through what we're walking through. When changes, troubles, and worries leave you scrambling and unsure of which way to turn, look to him and remember this:

My Scripture of Hope

Trust in him at all times, you people; pour out your hearts to him, for God is our refuge.

PSALM 62:8

_____
_____
_____
_____
_____

My Anxious Thoughts to Release

_____
_____
_____

God's Promise to Me

I can open my heart to Jesus. I can be specific about my fears.
He will understand because he has felt all of this too.

My Prayer

_____
_____

In the Storms

We have placed our confidence in him, and
he will continue to rescue us.

2 Corinthians 1:10 nlt

Peter and his fellow storm riders knew they were in trouble. "But the boat was now in the middle of the sea, tossed by the waves, for the wind was contrary" (Matthew 14:24 nkjv).

What should have been a sixty-minute cruise became a nightlong battle. The boat lurched and lunged like a kite in a March wind. Winds whipped the sails, leaving the disciples "in the middle of the sea, tossed by the waves." Apt description, perhaps, for your stage in life? Perhaps all we need to do is substitute a couple of nouns.

In the middle of a divorce, tossed about by guilt.

In the middle of debt, tossed about by creditors.

In the middle of a recession, tossed about by inflation.

The disciples fought the storm for nine cold, skin-drenching hours. And at about 4:00 a.m., the unspeakable happened. They spotted someone coming on the water. "'A ghost!' they said, crying out in terror" (Matthew 14:26 msg).

They didn't expect Jesus to come to them this way.

Neither do we. But it is in storms that he does his finest work, for it is in storms that he has our keenest attention.

We talk about Jesus being with us always, but do we believe? Do we expect to see him in our storms? The crashing waves and howling winds may blind us to his presence, but don't doubt that he is there. When storms are threatening to capsize you, remember this:

My Scripture of Hope

"When you pass through the waters, I will be with you. When you cross rivers, you will not drown. When you walk through fire, you will not be burned, nor will the flames hurt you. This is because I, the LORD, am your God, the Holy One of Israel, your Savior."

ISAIAH 43:2–3 NCV

_____

_____

_____

_____

_____

_____

My Anxious Thoughts to Release

_____

_____

_____

God's Promise to Me

I can expect to see Jesus in my storms. He is with me. He will guide me to peaceful waters.

My Prayer

_____

_____

No End in Sight

This is how we know what real love is: Jesus gave his life for us.
1 JOHN 3:16 NCV

It's nice to be included. You aren't always. Universities exclude you if you aren't smart enough. Businesses exclude you if you aren't qualified enough, and sadly, some churches exclude you if you aren't good enough.

But though they may exclude you, Christ includes you. When asked to describe the width of his love, he stretched one hand to the right and the other to the left and had them nailed in that position so you would know he died loving you.

But isn't there a limit? Surely there has to be an end to this love. You'd think so, wouldn't you? But David the adulterer never found it. Paul the murderer never found it. Peter the liar never found it. When it came to life, they hit bottom. But when it came to God's love, they never did.

How wide is God's love? Wide enough for the whole world. Are you included in the world? Then you are included in God's love.

When it comes to worry, it can sometimes feel as if there is no end in sight. As soon as one issue is resolved, another pops up to take its place. The worry we thought we'd gotten rid of pours in again. But the thing that is truly endless isn't worry; it's the love of Christ. When you need a reminder of just how vast his love is, remember this:

My Scripture of Hope

I am convinced that neither death nor life, neither angels nor
demons, neither the present nor the future, nor any powers,
neither height nor depth, nor anything else in all creation,
will be able to separate us from the love of God that is in
Christ Jesus our Lord.

ROMANS 8:38–39

_____

_____

_____

_____

_____

_____

My Anxious Thoughts to Release

_____

_____

_____

God's Promise to Me

There is no limit to the love of Christ. It stretches beyond
infinity. And it surrounds, fills, and embraces me.

My Prayer

_____

_____

There He Is

"I the LORD do not change."
MALACHI 3:6

I suspect the most consistent thing about life has to be its inconsistency. Don't all of us live with a fear of the unknown? It's this eerie inconsistency that keeps all of us living on the edge of our chairs.

Yet it was in this inconsistency that God had his finest hour. Never did the good in the world so intertwine with the bad as it did on the cross. God on a cross. Humanity at its worst. Divinity at its best.

God is not stumped by an evil world. He doesn't gasp in amazement at the depth of our faith or the depth of our failures. He knows the condition of the world and loves it just the same. For just when we find a place where God would never be (like on a cross), we look again and there he is, in the flesh.

The peace of God transcends all logic, scheming, and efforts to explain it. This kind of peace is not a human achievement. It is a gift from above (John 14:27). The peace that kept his thoughts clear and heart pure as he hung on the cross. This was his peace. This can be your peace.

A life of faith does not guarantee immunity to troubles. This world is an ever-changing place, and those changes are not always what we hope they will be. But while life may change, God's faithfulness to us does not. When worries leave you craving his constancy in this inconsistent world, remember this:

My Scripture of Hope

"For God so loved the world that he gave his one and only Son, that whoever believes in him shall not perish but have eternal life."

JOHN 3:16

_____

_____

_____

_____

_____

_____

_____

My Anxious Thoughts to Release

_____

_____

_____

God's Promise to Me

God does not change. His love does not change. His promises do not change. When I look for him, he will be found. When I need him, he is already there.

My Prayer

_____

_____

Don't Be Fooled by the Fog

Forgetting those things which are behind and reaching forward
to those things which are ahead, I press toward the goal.
PHILIPPIANS 3:13–14 NKJV

In 1952, Florence Chadwick attempted to swim the chilly ocean waters between Catalina Island and the California shore. She swam through foggy weather and choppy seas for fifteen hours. Her muscles began to cramp, and her resolve weakened. She begged to be taken out of the water, but her mother, riding in a boat alongside, urged her not to give up. She kept trying but grew exhausted and stopped swimming. Aides lifted her out of the water and into the boat. They paddled a few more minutes, the mist broke, and she discovered that the shore was less than a half mile away. "All I could see was the fog," she explained at a news conference. "I think if I could have seen the shore, I would have made it."[1]

Take a long look at the shore that awaits you. Don't be fooled by the fog of the slump. The finish may be only strokes away. Angels may be assembling, saints gathering, demons trembling. Stay at it! Stay in the water. Stay in the race. Look to the shore.

Foggy weather and choppy seas. That's an accurate way to describe how our days can look. It's tough to keep swimming when we can't see the shore. But we know, from hard experience, that with giving up comes regret. When our struggles exceed our strength, let's remember this:

My Scripture of Hope

"I am he, I am he who will sustain you. I have made you and
I will carry you; I will sustain you and I will rescue you."
ISAIAH 46:4

_____

_____

_____

_____

_____

_____

_____

_____

My Anxious Thoughts to Release

_____

_____

_____

God's Promise to Me

The Lord is the Master of all life's seas. He will keep
me from going under. He will get me to the shore.

My Prayer

_____

_____

For Thirsty Souls

*"If anyone thirsts, let him come to Me and drink. He
who believes in Me, as the Scripture has said, out
of his heart will flow rivers of living water."*

JOHN 7:37–38 NKJV

Don't you need regular sips from God's reservoir? I do. In countless situations—stressful meetings, dull days, long drives, demanding trips—and many times a day, I step to the underground spring of God. There I receive anew his work for my sin and death, the energy of his Spirit, his lordship, and his love.

Drink with me from his bottomless well. You don't have to live with a dehydrated heart.

Receive Christ's work on the cross, the energy of his Spirit, his lordship over your life, and his unending, unfailing love.

Don't you need a drink? Don't you long to flush out the fear, anxiety, and guilt? You can. Note the audience of his invitation. "If *anyone* thirsts, let him come to Me and drink" (v. 37 NKJV, emphasis mine). Are you *anyone*? If so, then step up to the well. You qualify for his water.

Drink deeply and often. And out of you will flow rivers of living water.

Fear, anxiety, guilt—they sap our strength and parch our soul. We've tried to quench our thirst with other "waters," but nothing satisfies. Nothing except Jesus. When you need the refreshing and reviving power of his living water, remember this:

My Scripture of Hope

"Whoever drinks the water I give them will never thirst. Indeed, the water I give them will become in them a spring of water welling up to eternal life."

JOHN 4:14

_____

_____

_____

_____

_____

_____

_____

_____

_____

My Anxious Thoughts to Release

_____

_____

_____

God's Promise to Me

I am invited to drink the living water of Christ's salvation. His Spirit will water, refresh, and revive my soul.

My Prayer

_____

_____

Take a Swing at Your Giant

The battle is the LORD's.
1 SAMUEL 17:47 NKJV

David . . . runs toward the army to meet Goliath (1 Samuel 17:48). Goliath throws back his head in laughter, just enough to shift his helmet and expose a square inch of forehead flesh. David spots the target and seizes the moment. The sound of the swirling sling is the only sound in the valley. *Ssshhhww. Ssshhhww. Ssshhhww.* The stone torpedoes through the air and into the skull; Goliath's eyes cross and legs buckle. He crumples to the ground and dies. David runs over and yanks Goliath's sword from its sheath, shish-kebabs the Philistine, and cuts off his head.

You might say that David knew how to get *a head* of his giant.

When was the last time you did the same? How long since you ran toward your challenge? We tend to retreat, duck behind a desk of work, or crawl into a nightclub of distraction or a bed of forbidden love. For a moment, a day, or a year, we feel safe, insulated, anesthetized, but then the work runs out, the liquor wears off, or the lover leaves, and we hear Goliath again. Booming. Bombastic.

Try a different tack. Rush your giant with a God-saturated soul. *Giant of divorce, you aren't entering my home! Giant of anxiety? It may take a lifetime, but you won't conquer me. Giant of worry, fear, doubt . . . you're going down.* How long since you loaded your sling and took a swing at your giant?

There are days we feel surrounded by giants. Insecurities and doubts and worries flood our minds and leave us shaking. But no giant is a match for our God. When our ears ring with the bellows of giants, take a swing at them by remembering this:

My Scripture of Hope

I sought the LORD, and he answered me; he delivered me from all my fears.

PSALM 34:4

_____

_____

_____

_____

My Anxious Thoughts to Release

_____

_____

_____

God's Promise to Me

God is greater than any giant in my life. Nothing and no one can defeat him. Because he fights for me, I can live free.

My Prayer

_____

_____

Sealed and Shielded

When you believed, you were marked in him
with a seal, the promised Holy Spirit.
EPHESIANS 1:13

T he most famous New Testament "sealing" occurred with the tomb of Jesus. Roman soldiers rolled a rock over the entrance and "set a seal on the stone" (Matthew 27:66 NASB). Archaeologists envision two ribbons stretched in front of the entrance, glued together with hardened wax that bore the imprimatur of the Roman government—SPQR (*Senatus Populusque Romanus*)—as if to say, "Stay away! The contents of this tomb belong to Rome." Their seal, of course, proved futile.

The seal of the Spirit, however, proves forceful. When you accepted Christ, God sealed you with the Spirit. "When you believed, you were marked in him with a seal, the promised Holy Spirit." When hell's interlopers come seeking to snatch you from God, the seal turns them away. God paid too high a price to leave you unguarded.

You are "shielded by God's power" (1 Peter 1:5). The Holy Spirit pours the love *of* God in our hearts, not love *for* God. You belong to the Father. *Signed, sealed, and soon-to-be delivered.*

There are days when the worries of the world pull and tear at us. We feel as battered and broken as the disciples hiding in that locked room, mourning their crucified Savior. But the world isn't as powerful as it leads us to believe. Its seals couldn't hold our Savior. But his seal holds us and never lets us go. Remember this:

My Scripture of Hope

"I give them eternal life, and they shall never perish; no one will snatch them out of my hand. My Father, who has given them to me, is greater than all; no one can snatch them out of my Father's hand."

JOHN 10:28–29

_____

_____

_____

_____

_____

_____

My Anxious Thoughts to Release

_____

_____

_____

God's Promise to Me

I was bought—redeemed and sealed—by Christ. I belong to him. He protects me with his Spirit who lives in me. This world cannot snatch me away from him.

My Prayer

_____

_____

A Different Point of View

I have learned in whatever state I am, to be content.

PHILIPPIANS 4:11 NKJV

In his book *Money: A User's Manual*, Bob Russell describes a farmer who once grew discontent with his farm. He griped about the lake on his property always needing to be stocked and managed. The hills humped up his roads, forcing him to drive up and down. And those fat cows lumbered through his pasture. All the fencing and feeding—what a headache!

He called a Realtor and made plans to list the farm. A few days later the agent phoned, wanting approval for the advertisement she intended to place in the local paper. She read the ad to the farmer. It described a lovely farm in an ideal location—quiet and peaceful, contoured with rolling hills, carpeted with soft meadows, nourished by a fresh lake, and blessed with well-bred livestock. The farmer said, "Read that ad to me again."

After hearing it a second time, he decided, "I've changed my mind. I'm not going to sell. I've been looking for a place like that all my life."

Examine your perspective toward life. Before you make a change, be careful. Consult your design. Consult your Designer.

> What would an outsider write about our lives? Would they see a bevy of blessings that worry and stress cause us to overlook? When we need fresh eyes—a fresh perspective—on our lives, let's remember this:

My Scripture of Hope

God is able to bless you abundantly, so that in all things at all times, having all that you need, you will abound in every good work.

2 CORINTHIANS 9:8

My Anxious Thoughts to Release

God's Promise to Me

I am a child of God. He put me in this time and place for a purpose. He has filled this time and place with his presence and his provision. With his help, I can see the blessings he has given me.

My Prayer

A Daily Habit

As soon as I pray, you answer me; you
encourage me by giving me strength.
PSALM 138:3 NLT

Rejoice *in* this day? God invites us to. As Paul rejoiced *in* prison; David wrote psalms *in* the wilderness; Jonah prayed *in* the fish's belly; Paul and Silas sang *in* jail; Shadrach, Meshach, and Abednego remained resolute *in* the fiery furnace; John saw heaven *in* his exile; and Jesus prayed *in* his garden of pain. Could we rejoice smack-dab *in* the midst of this day? Imagine the difference if we could.

Suppose that when you're neck-deep in a terrible day, you resolve to give it a chance. You choose not to drink or work or worry it away but give it a fair shake. You trust more. Stress less. Amplify gratitude. Mute grumbling. And what do you know? Before long the day is done and surprisingly decent.

So decent, in fact, that you resolve to give the next day the same fighting chance. It arrives with its hang-ups and bang-ups, bird droppings and shirt stains, but by and large, by golly, giving the day a chance works! You do the same the next day and the next. Days become a week. Weeks become months. Months become years of good days.

In such a fashion good lives are built. One good day at a time.

We slip into habits so easily, even the habit of having bad days. Too many troubles in a row, and we begin expecting things to go wrong. Worrying *before* they do. Could we try a new habit? A habit of looking for hope? Remember this:

My Scripture of Hope

You will teach me how to live a holy life. Being with you will fill me with joy; at your right hand I will find pleasure forever.

PSALM 16:11 NCV

_____
_____
_____
_____
_____
_____
_____
_____

My Anxious Thoughts to Release

_____
_____
_____

God's Promise to Me

Each day is God's new creation. It is shining with hope just waiting to be found. He will help me find it.

My Prayer

_____
_____

"I Am" in the Storm

Jesus Christ is the same yesterday, today, and forever.
HEBREWS 13:8 NCV

I am God's Son" (John 10:36 NCV).

"I am the resurrection and the life" (John 11:25 NCV).

"I am the way, and the truth, and the life" (John 14:6 NCV).

"I am the true vine" (John 15:1 NCV).

The present-tense Christ. He never says, "I was." We do. We do because "we were." We were younger, faster, prettier. Prone to be people of the past tense, we reminisce. Not God. Unwavering in strength, he need never say, "I was."

From the center of the storm, the unwavering Jesus shouts, "I am." Tall in the wreckage of war and terrorism. Bold against the Galilean waves. ICU, battlefield, boardroom, prison cell, or maternity ward—whatever your storm, "I am."

God gets into things! Red Seas. Big fish. Lions' dens and furnaces. Bankrupt businesses and jail cells. Judean wildernesses, weddings, funerals, and Galilean tempests. Look and you'll find what everyone from Moses to Martha discovered. God in the middle of our storms.

That includes yours.

We have our own set of "I am" statements, don't we? We pull them out when the storms threaten. *I am worried. I am afraid. I am exhausted. I am at the end of my rope.* When your "I ams" are swirling like a tempest and you need a reminder of the great I AM, remember this:

My Scripture of Hope

My dear children, you belong to God and have defeated them; because God's Spirit, who is in you, is greater than the devil, who is in the world.

1 JOHN 4:4 NCV

_____
_____
_____
_____
_____
_____
_____
_____

My Anxious Thoughts to Release

_____
_____
_____

God's Promise to Me

The true I AM is greater than all my worried "I ams."
He is with me in this storm. He is the same Savior who
defeated the devil. He is here and fighting for me.

My Prayer

_____
_____

At Home in His Love

"Abide in My love."
JOHN 15:9 NKJV

When you abide somewhere, you live there. You grow familiar with the surroundings. You don't pull in the driveway and ask, "Where is the garage?" You don't consult the blueprint to find the kitchen. To abide is to be at home.

To abide in Christ's love is to make his love your home. Not a roadside park or hotel room you occasionally visit, but your preferred dwelling. You rest in him. Eat in him. When thunder claps, you step beneath his roof. His walls secure you from the winds. His fireplace warms you from the winters of life. As John urged, "We take up permanent residence in a life of love" (1 John 4:17 MSG).

You abandon the old house of false love and move into his home of real love.

Our aim—our only aim—is to be at home in Christ. He is our permanent mailing address. He is our place of refuge and security. We are comfortable in his presence, free to be our authentic selves.

It takes only one experience with false love to doubt our welcome and our worth. Even with God. Though we might wear out our welcome in other places, we can linger in Christ for eternity. He has invited us in. He *wants* us to be where he is. When you need a reminder of where your true home lies, remember this:

My Scripture of Hope

"Father, I want those you have given me to be with me where I am, and to see my glory, the glory you have given me because you loved me before the creation of the world."

JOHN 17:24

_____
_____
_____
_____
_____
_____
_____
_____
_____

My Anxious Thoughts to Release

_____
_____
_____

God's Promise to Me

Jesus has prepared a place for me. He invites me
into his presence. He wants me where he is.

My Prayer

_____
_____

Out of Gas

The eyes of the LORD are on the righteous, and
His ears are open to their prayers.

1 PETER 3:12 NKJV

What do you do when you run out of gas? All of us run out of something. You need kindness, but the gauge is on empty. You need hope, but the needle is in the red. You want five gallons of solutions but can only muster a few drops. What do you do? Stare at the gauge? Deny the problem?

No. Worry won't start the car. Fear doesn't fuel an engine. Denial doesn't bump the needle. In the case of an empty tank, we've learned to get the car to a gas pump ASAP.

My first thought when I run out of fuel is, *How can I get this car to a gas pump?* Your first thought when you have a problem should be, *How can I get this problem to Jesus?*

Instead of starting with what you have (or don't have), start with Jesus. Start with his wealth, his resources, and his strength. Count the number of times Jesus has helped you face the impossible. Before you lash out in fear, look up in faith. Take a moment. Turn to your Father for help.

Here's the question: What do we do when we run out of gas? Where do we go to fill our tanks? Food? Social media? Work? Or do we go to the open-all-night station of Jesus? When you're running on fumes—with nothing left to give—remember this:

My Scripture of Hope

Yes, my soul, find rest in God; my hope comes from him.
Truly he is my rock and my salvation; he is my fortress, I will
not be shaken.

PSALM 62:5–6

_____

_____

_____

_____

_____

_____

_____

_____

My Anxious Thoughts to Release

_____

_____

_____

God's Promise to Me

Jesus is the solution to every problem, the answer to
every question. He will fill me with all I need.

My Prayer

_____

_____

Second Chances

"I came to give life—life in all its fullness."
JOHN 10:10 NCV

Not many second chances exist in the world today. Just ask the kid who didn't make the Little League team, the fellow who got the pink slip, or the mother of three who got dumped for a "pretty little thing."

Not many second chances. Nowadays it's more like "It's now or never." "Around here we don't tolerate incompetence." "Gotta get tough to get along." "Not much room at the top." "Three strikes and you're out." "It's a dog-eat-dog world!"

Jesus would say, "Then don't live with the dogs." That makes sense, doesn't it? Why let a bunch of other failures tell you how much of a failure you are?

It's not every day that you find someone who will give you a second chance—much less someone who will give you a second chance every day. But in Jesus, you find both.

Failure, betrayal, sickness, disappointment—they cannot take our joy, because they cannot take our Jesus. What you have in Christ is greater than anything you don't have in life. In Christ you have a second chance.

But the devil would love for us to forget that. He wants us to believe there are no second chances. He wants us to worry about it, to be afraid. When you need a reminder of the truth, remember this:

My Scripture of Hope

"For God did not send his Son into the world to condemn the
world, but to save the world through him."

JOHN 3:17

_____
_____
_____
_____
_____
_____
_____
_____
_____

My Anxious Thoughts to Release

_____
_____
_____

God's Promise to Me

God gives second chances. Each day is a new beginning.
And he has filled it with both blessings and plans for me.

My Prayer

_____
_____

What Thoughts Are
You Thinking?

Be careful what you think, because your thoughts run your life.
PROVERBS 4:23 NCV

D o you let anyone who knocks on your door enter your house?
Don't let every thought that surfaces dwell in your mind. Take
it captive; make it obey Jesus. If it refuses, don't think it.

Negative thoughts never strengthen you. How many times have
you cleared a traffic jam with your grumbles? Does groaning about
bills make them disappear? Why moan about your aches and pains,
problems and tasks?

"Be careful what you think, because your thoughts run your life"
(Proverbs 4:23 NCV). Do you want to be happy tomorrow? Then sow
seeds of happiness today. (Count blessings. Memorize Bible verses.
Pray. Sing hymns. Spend time with encouraging people.)

Healthy thinking is good medicine for anxiety.

Be intentional with your thoughts. The Bible tells us to take every
thought captive (2 Corinthians 10:5), but it also tells us we don't
have to do all that rounding up on our own (Philippians 4:13).
When you need help finding your way back to the bright side,
remember this:

My Scripture of Hope

You, LORD, keep my lamp burning; my God turns my darkness into light.

PSALM 18:28

_____

_____

_____

_____

_____

_____

_____

_____

My Anxious Thoughts to Release

_____

_____

_____

God's Promise to Me

The Lord is my strength. He will help me take these
worrisome thoughts captive. His light will lead
me out of the darkness and closer to him.

My Prayer

_____

_____

Under His Wings

He will cover you with his feathers, and under his wings you can hide.
PSALM 91:4 NCV

My college friends and I barely escaped a West Texas storm before it pummeled the park where we were spending a Saturday afternoon. As we were leaving, my buddy brought the car to a sudden stop and gestured to a tender sight on the ground. A mother bird sat exposed to the rain, her wing extended over her baby who had fallen out of the nest. The fierce storm prohibited her from returning to the tree, so she covered her child until the wind passed.

From how many winds is God protecting you? His wing, at this moment, shields you. A slanderous critic heading toward your desk is interrupted by a phone call. A burglar en route to your house has a flat tire. A drunk driver runs out of gas before your car passes his. God, your guardian, protects you.

He can give you a happiness that can never be taken, a grace that will never expire, and a wisdom that will ever increase. Protection you may never even realize this side of heaven. He is a fountain of living hope that will never be exhausted.

> While we may feel the stormy winds of the world whipping in our faces, God never once leaves us unguarded. And one day, on the other side of this life, we will know all the protection God has provided us. Until then, we catch glimpses of him. If you're weary and needing the shelter of the wings, remember this:

My Scripture of Hope

The LORD watches over you—the LORD is your shade at your right hand; the sun will not harm you by day, nor the moon by night. The LORD will keep you from all harm—he will watch over your life; the LORD will watch over your coming and going both now and forevermore.

PSALM 121:5–8

_____
_____
_____
_____
_____

My Anxious Thoughts to Release

_____
_____
_____

God's Promise to Me

God never ceases to watch over me. He guards me, shelters me, defends me. Nothing will touch me that he cannot handle. I am safe in the shadow of his wings.

My Prayer

_____
_____

Live Today

*"Your heavenly Father already knows all your needs. Seek
the Kingdom of God above all else, and live righteously,
and he will give you everything you need."*
MATTHEW 6:32–33 NLT

An hour is too short, a year too long. Days are the bite-size portions of life, the God-designed segments of life management. Eighty-four thousand heartbeats. One thousand four hundred and forty minutes. A complete rotation of the earth. Both a sunrise and a sunset. A brand-spanking-new, unsoiled, untouched, uncharted, and unused day! A gift of twenty-four unlived, unexplored hours.

And if you can stack one good day on another and another, you will link together a good life. But here's what you need to keep in mind.

You no longer have yesterday. It slipped away as you slept. It is gone. You'll more easily retrieve a puff of smoke. You can't change, alter, or improve it. Sorry, no mulligans allowed.

You do not yet have tomorrow. Unless you accelerate the orbit of the earth or convince the sun to rise twice before it sets once, you can't live tomorrow today. You can't spend tomorrow's money, celebrate tomorrow's achievements, or resolve tomorrow's riddles. You have only today. This is the day the Lord has made. Live in it. You must be present to win.

Being "present" isn't as easy as it sounds. Our minds so easily wander back to the *could haves* and *should haves* of yesterday and don't stop until they crash right into the *what ifs* and *what might happens* of tomorrow. When past regrets and future worries are stealing your today, remember this:

My Scripture of Hope

The faithful love of the LORD never ends! His mercies never cease. Great is his faithfulness; his mercies begin afresh each morning. I say to myself, "The LORD is my inheritance; therefore, I will hope in him!"

LAMENTATIONS 3:22–24 NLT

_____
_____
_____
_____
_____
_____
_____

My Anxious Thoughts to Release

_____
_____
_____

God's Promise to Me

The past is covered by God's grace. The future is in his hands. Today is the day I can live—and I can live every moment in his presence.

My Prayers

_____
_____

The Spirit Pleads for Us

The Spirit helps us in our weakness.
ROMANS 8:26 NET

I n the ultimate declaration of communion, God called himself
Immanuel, which means "God with us." He became flesh. He
became sin. He defeated the grave. He is still with us. In the form of
his Spirit, he comforts, teaches, and convicts.

"The Spirit helps us in our weakness." What a sentence worthy of
a highlighter. Who does not need this reminder? Weak bodies. Weak
wills. Weakened resolves. We've known them all. The word *weakness*
can refer to physical infirmities, as with the invalid who had been
unable to walk for thirty-eight years (John 5:5), or spiritual impo-
tence, as with the spiritually "helpless" of Romans 5:6 (NASB).

Whether we are feeble of soul or body or both, how good to know
it's not up to us. The Spirit himself is pleading for us.

Do not assume God is watching from a distance. Avoid the quick-
sand that bears the marker "God has left you!" Do not indulge this
lie. It's one thing to face a challenge, but to face it alone? Isolation
creates a downward cycle of fret and fear. Choose instead to be the
person who clutches the presence of God with both hands. When
you need a reminder that you are not alone, remember this:

My Scripture of Hope

"If you love me, keep my commands. And I will ask the Father, and he will give you another advocate to help you and be with you forever—the Spirit of truth."

JOHN 14:15–17

_____
_____
_____
_____
_____
_____
_____
_____
_____

My Anxious Thoughts to Release

_____
_____
_____

God's Promise to Me

The Lord is with me. His Spirit lives in me. I have nothing to fear. Because he who is in me is greater than anything in this world.

My Prayer

_____
_____

Store Up the Sweet

*Whatever is true, whatever is honorable . . . if there is
anything worthy of praise, think about these things.*
PHILIPPIANS 4:8 RSV

Change the thoughts, and you change the person. If today's thoughts are tomorrow's actions, what happens when we fill our minds with thoughts of God's love? Will standing beneath the downpour of his grace change the way we feel about others?

Paul says absolutely! It's not enough to keep the bad stuff out. We've got to let the good stuff in. It's not enough to keep no list of wrongs. We have to cultivate a list of blessings: "Whatever is true, whatever is honorable, whatever is just, whatever is pure, whatever is lovely, whatever is gracious, if there is any excellence, if there is anything worthy of praise, think about these things" (RSV). *Thinking* conveys the idea of pondering—studying and focusing, allowing what is viewed to have an impact on us.

Rather than store up the sour, store up the sweet. Listen. You have not been sprinkled with forgiveness. You have not been spattered with grace. You have not been dusted with kindness. You have been immersed in it. You are submerged in mercy. You are a minnow in the ocean of his mercy. Let it change you!

Count your blessings. It's a trite old saying, yet still we try to do as we're advised. But the counting falters when a memory pops up or a worry creeps in. Why does it seem that the sour experiences so easily chase away the sweet? When you need a reminder of the good in your life, remember this:

My Scripture of Hope

You are a chosen people, royal priests, a holy nation, a people
for God's own possession. You were chosen to tell about the
wonderful acts of God, who called you out of darkness into
his wonderful light.

1 PETER 2:9 NCV

_____

_____

_____

_____

_____

_____

_____

My Anxious Thoughts to Release

_____

_____

_____

God's Promise to Me

I am chosen. I am a child of God. He called
me out of darkness into his light.

My Prayer

_____

_____

It's Going to Turn Out All Right

"Don't be afraid," he said. "Take courage. I am here!"
MATTHEW 14:27 NLT

God's call to courage is not a call to naïveté or ignorance. We aren't to be oblivious to the overwhelming challenges that life brings. "We must pay much closer attention to what we have heard, so that we do not drift away from it" (Hebrews 2:1 NASB). Do whatever it takes to keep your gaze on Jesus.

When a friend of mine spent several days in the hospital at the bedside of her husband, she relied on hymns to keep her spirits up. Every few minutes, she stepped into the restroom and sang a few verses of "Great Is Thy Faithfulness." Do likewise! Memorize Scripture. Read biographies of great lives. Ponder the testimonies of faithful Christians. Make the deliberate decision to set your hope on him.

As followers of God, you and I have a huge asset. We know everything is going to turn out all right. Christ hasn't budged from his throne, and Romans 8:28 hasn't evaporated from the Bible. Our problems have always been his possibilities.

Feed your fears, and your faith will starve.

Feed your faith, and your fears will.

We know everything is going to turn out all right. That's the promise of Romans 8:28. But it's hard to remember when all the possibilities of what could go wrong are swirling around us. When fear is plentiful, let's fix our gaze on Jesus and remember this:

My Scripture of Hope

We know that all things work together for good to those who love God, to those who are the called according to His purpose.

ROMANS 8:28 NKJV

_____
_____
_____
_____
_____
_____
_____

My Anxious Thoughts to Release

_____
_____
_____

God's Promise to Me

The Lord is in control. He knows how it all turns out.
And he promised it will be for my good. He will give me
the courage to keep going and the hope to hold on.

My Prayer

_____
_____

Jesus Knows

"I am the one God chose and sent into the world."
JOHN 10:36 NCV

God is with us.

He knows hurt. His siblings called him crazy. He knows hunger. He made a meal out of wheat-field grains.

He knows exhaustion. So sleepy, he dozed in a storm-tossed boat.

He knows betrayal. He gave Judas three years of love. Judas, in turn, gave Jesus a betrayer's kiss.

Most of all, he knows sin. Not his own, mind you. But he knows yours. Every lie you've told. Person you've hurt. Promise you've broken. Virtue you've abandoned. Opportunity you've squandered.

Every deed you've committed against God—for all sin is against God—Jesus knows. He knows them better than you do. He knows their price. Because he paid it.

Christ takes away your sin, and in doing so, he takes away your commonness. No longer need you say, "No one knows me." God knows you. He engraved your name on his hands and keeps your tears in a bottle (Isaiah 49:16; Psalm 56:8 NASB). God knows you.

Jesus knows *everything*. Every last detail about every last little thing we've tried to forget, cover up, and hide. And still he chose to purchase us with his own suffering and sorrow. We don't ever have to be afraid of him, of losing his love, of losing his presence. If you need reminding of how much he thinks you're worth, remember this:

My Scripture of Hope

He personally carried our sins in his body on the cross so that
we can be dead to sin and live for what is right. By his wounds
you are healed.

1 PETER 2:24 NLT

_____
_____
_____
_____
_____
_____
_____
_____
_____

My Anxious Thoughts to Release

_____
_____
_____

God's Promise to Me

I am fully and completely known by Jesus. He chose to die for
my sins anyway. I cannot lose his love. He will not abandon me.

My Prayer

_____
_____

The First Step

Anyone who is having troubles should pray.
JAMES 5:13 NCV

Have you taken your disappointments to God? You've shared them with your neighbor, your relatives, your friends. But have you taken them to God? "Anyone who is having troubles should pray."

Before you go anywhere else with your disappointments, go to God.

Maybe you don't want to trouble God with your hurts. *After all, he's got famines and pestilence and wars; he won't care about my little struggles,* you think. Why don't you let him decide that? He cared enough about a wedding to provide the wine. He cared enough about Peter's tax payment to give him a coin. He cared enough about the woman at the well to give her answers. "He cares about you" (1 Peter 5:7 NCV).

Your first step is to go to the right person. Go to God.

God said, "Call on me in the day of trouble" (Psalm 50:15).

Jesus said, "Ask, and it will be given to you; seek, and you will find; knock, and it will be opened to you" (Matthew 7:7 NKJV). There is no uncertainty in that promise. No "might," "perhaps," or "possibly will." Jesus states unflinchingly that when you ask, he listens.

Fear triggers either despair or prayer. Choose wisely.

When things go wrong, we often turn to friends, or social media, or our own attempts to fix whatever problem has come our way. We turn to all those who are just as powerless as we are to do anything about the problem. What if we tried a different approach? When the day is filled with disappointment, and you're in need of hope, remember this:

My Scripture of Hope

The LORD hears his people when they call to him for help. He rescues them from all their troubles.

PSALM 34:17 NLT

My Anxious Thoughts to Release

God's Promise to Me

When I call to God, he will answer. I can
entrust my disappointments to him because he
cares about me. He will rescue me.

My Prayer

No Spirit of Fear

God has not given us a spirit of fear, but of
power and of love and of a sound mind.
2 TIMOTHY 1:7 NKJV

Fear never wrote a symphony or poem, negotiated a peace treaty, or cured a disease. Fear never pulled a family out of poverty or a country out of bigotry. Fear never saved a marriage or a business. Courage did that. Faith did that. People who refused to consult or cower to their timidities did those things.

To be clear, fear serves a healthy function. It is the canary in the coal mine, warning of potential danger. Fear is the appropriate reaction to a burning building or growling dog. Fear itself is not a sin. But it can lead to sin.

If we medicate fear with angry outbursts, drinking binges, sullen withdrawals, self-starvation, or viselike control, we exclude God from the solution and exacerbate the problem. We subject ourselves to a position of fear, allowing anxiety to dominate and define our lives. Joy-sapping worries. Day-numbing dread. Repeated bouts of insecurity that petrify and paralyze us. Hysteria is not from God. "For God has not given us a *spirit* of fear" (2 Timothy 1:7 NKJV, emphasis mine).

Fear may fill our world, but it doesn't have to fill our hearts. It will always knock on the door. Just don't invite it in for dinner, and for heaven's sake, don't offer it a bed for the night.

We certainly don't mean to, but it happens. We open the door, just a crack, and anxiety creeps in. He's not a considerate guest. He doesn't care that his companionship stinks. He invites his freeloading pals—worry and fear—over to crash on the couch. When you need help kicking this crew to the curb, remember this:

My Scripture of Hope

The eyes of the LORD search the whole earth in order to strengthen those whose hearts are fully committed to him.
2 CHRONICLES 16:9 NLT

My Anxious Thoughts to Release

God's Promise to Me

God's Spirit within me is greater than any anxiety, any worry, any fear. I can turn to him, and he will strengthen me. He will show me what is real and what is true.

My Prayer

The Christ of Your Mondays

I can do all things through Christ who strengthens me.

PHILIPPIANS 4:13 NKJV

Stand and consider:

- The Hubble Space Telescope sends back infrared images of faint galaxies that are perhaps twelve billion light-years away (twelve billion times six trillion miles).
- Astronomers venture a feeble estimate that the number of stars in the universe equals the number of grains of sand on all the beaches of the world.[2]
- The star Betelgeuse has a diameter of 700 million miles, which is larger than the earth's orbit around the sun.[3]

Why the immensity? Why such vast, unmeasured, unexplored, "unused" space? So that you and I, freshly stunned, could be stirred by this resolve: "I can do all things through Christ who strengthens me."

The Christ of the galaxies is the Christ of your Mondays. The Starmaker manages your travel schedule. Relax. You have a friend in high places.

What is it about Mondays that so often knocks the stuffing out of us? Is it the end of the weekend? Or the fact that weekday time is so rarely our own? Or perhaps it's the anxiety born of all the unknowns this week will hold. When you need a reminder of who created and controls each day, remember this:

My Scripture of Hope

May you have the power to understand, as all God's people should, how wide, how long, how high, and how deep his love is.

EPHESIANS 3:18 NLT

_____

_____

_____

_____

_____

_____

_____

My Anxious Thoughts to Release

_____

_____

_____

God's Promise to Me

The God who made the stars watches over me. He knows my name. He knows all that is coming my way. And he will enable me to do all that truly needs to be done.

My Prayer

_____

_____

A Love That Never Fails

Love never fails.

1 CORINTHIANS 13:8

First Corinthians 13 is the Mount Everest of love writings. And no verses get to the heart of the chapter like verses 4 through 8.

> Love is patient, love is kind. It does not envy, it does not boast, it is not proud. It does not dishonor others, it is not self-seeking, it is not easily angered, it keeps no record of wrongs. Love does not delight in evil but rejoices with the truth. It always protects, always trusts, always hopes, always perseveres. Love never fails.

Rather than let this scripture remind us of a love we cannot produce, let it remind us of a love we cannot resist—God's love.

Some of you are so thirsty for this type of love. Those who should have loved you didn't. Those who could have loved you didn't. You were left at the hospital. Left at the altar. Left with an empty bed. Left with a broken heart. Left with your question "Does anybody love me?"

Please listen to heaven's answer. God loves you. Personally. Powerfully. Passionately. Others have promised and failed. But God has promised and succeeded. He loves you with an unfailing love. And his love—if you will let it—can fill you and leave you with a love worth giving. So come. Come thirsty and drink deeply.

> The devil has one goal: to lead us away from God. And where he leads us to is a sunless place, void of light and love. He wants us to believe that's all there is. His lies are exaggerated, overstated,

inflated, and irrational. *No one will ever love me. Everyone is against me.* All lies. No one is unloved or unlovable. When the devil's lies are fueling your anxious thoughts, remember this:

My Scripture of Hope

The LORD your God is living among you. . . . With his love, he will calm all your fears. He will rejoice over you with joyful songs.

ZEPHANIAH 3:17 NLT

My Anxious Thoughts to Release

God's Promise to Me

I am loved. Without end and without conditions.
God's love will never fail me.

My Prayer

When Worry Whispers

For the Lord God is a sun and shield; the Lord will give grace and glory; no good thing will He withhold from those who walk uprightly.

PSALM 84:11 NKJV

God says: "Every detail in our lives of love for God is worked into something good" (Romans 8:28 MSG).

Worry takes a look at catastrophes and groans, "It's all coming unraveled."

God's Word says, "[God has] done it all and done it well" (Mark 7:37 MSG).

Worry disagrees: "The world has gone crazy."

God's Word calls God "the blessed controller of all things" (1 Timothy 6:15 PHILLIPS).

Worry wonders if anyone is in control.

God's Word declares, "God will take care of everything you need" (Philippians 4:19 MSG).

Worry whispers this lie: "God doesn't know what you need."

God's Word reasons: "You're at least decent to your own children. So don't you think the God who conceived you in love will be even better?" (Matthew 7:11 MSG).

Worry discounts and replies, "You're on your own. It's you against the world."

Worry wages war on your faith. Worry forgets that God wins.

Worry whispers all sorts of lies about God, his Word, and who's really going to win. We know this, and yet when catastrophes and chaos crash all around us, it's hard not to listen. When worry comes chattering in your ear, remember this:

My Scripture of Hope

We know that in all things God works for the good of those who love him, who have been called according to his purpose.

ROMANS 8:28

_____

_____

_____

_____

My Anxious Thoughts to Release

_____

_____

_____

God's Promise to Me

God is in control. He's working in every detail of my life. He's working it all out for my good. And he's already won.

My Prayer

_____

_____

Slow Down and Rest

Six days you shall labor and do all your work, but the
seventh day is the Sabbath of the LORD your God. In it you
shall do no work: you, nor your son, nor your daughter.

EXODUS 20:9–10 NKJV

God knows us so well. He can see the store owner reading this verse and thinking, *Somebody needs to work that day. If I can't, my son will.* So God says, "Nor your son." *Then my daughter will.* "Nor your daughter." *I guess I'll have to send my cow to run the store, or maybe I'll find some stranger to help me.* "No," God says. "One day of the week you will say no to work and yes to worship. You will slow and sit down and lie down and rest."

Still we object: "What about my grades?" "I've got my sales quota." We offer up one reason after another, but God silences them all with a poignant reminder: "In six days the LORD made the heavens and the earth, the sea, and all that is in them, and rested the seventh day" (Exodus 20:11 NKJV). God's message is plain: "If creation didn't crash when I rested, it won't crash when you do."

Repeat these words after me: it is not my job to run the world.

The bow cannot always be bent without fear of breaking. For a field to bear fruit, it must occasionally lie fallow. And for you to be healthy, you must rest. Slow down, and God will heal you. He will bring rest to your mind, to your body, and most of all to your soul. He will lead you to green pastures.

Do you ever feel as if you can't stop? It's more than a feeling, isn't it? It's a fear. A fear that everything will come crashing down if we so much as pause to breathe. If we're not in complete control. That's the real issue. And when control slips away, our anxiety levels soar. Instead of seeking more control, let's relinquish it to the One who's really in control. When you need a reminder that it's okay to let go and rest, remember this:

My Scripture of Hope

He makes me lie down in green pastures, he leads me beside quiet waters, he refreshes my soul.

PSALM 23:2–3

_____

_____

_____

_____

My Anxious Thoughts to Release

_____

_____

_____

God's Promise to Me

God is in perfect control. I can trust him. I can rest in him.

My Prayer

_____

_____

The Pot of Prayer

I will go to the altar of God, to God who is my joy and happiness.
PSALM 43:4 NCV

L et's say a stress stirrer comes your way. The doctor decides you need an operation. She detects a lump and thinks it best that you have it removed. So there you are, walking out of her office. You've just been handed this cup of anxiety. What are you going to do with it? You can place it in one of two pots.

You can dump your bad news in the vat of worry and pull out the spoon. Turn on the fire. Stew on it. Stir it. Mope for a while. Brood for a time. Won't be long before you'll have a delightful pot of pessimism.

How about a different idea? The pot of prayer. Before the door of the doctor's office closes, give the problem to God. "I receive your lordship. Nothing comes to me that hasn't passed through you." In addition, stir in a healthy helping of gratitude. Remember the tax refund, the timely counsel, or the suddenly open seat on the overbooked flight. A glimpse into the past generates strength for the future.

Your part is prayer and gratitude. God's part? Peace and protection.

Believing prayer ushers in God's peace. Not a random, nebulous, earthly peace, but his peace. Imported from heaven. The same tranquility that marks the throne room, God offers to you.

Life hands us all manner of stress on a regular basis. It's easy to let our shoulders ache with the burden of challenges ranging from simple to severe. When you need less stress and more peace, remember this:

My Scripture of Hope

Do not be anxious about anything, but in every situation, by prayer and petition, with thanksgiving, present your requests to God. And the peace of God, which transcends all understanding, will guard your hearts and your minds in Christ Jesus.

PHILIPPIANS 4:6–7

_____
_____
_____
_____
_____

My Anxious Thoughts to Release

_____
_____

God's Promise to Me

God has already been to the end of this problem. His solution is coming. He will fill me with his peace while I await his answer.

My Prayer

_____
_____

His Idea

I will praise You, for I am fearfully and wonderfully made;
marvelous are Your works, and that my soul knows very well.
PSALM 139:14 NKJV

F ear of insignificance creates the result it dreads, arrives at the destination it tries to avoid, facilitates the scenario it disdains. If a basketball player stands at the foul line repeating, "I'll never make the shot, I'll never make the shot," guess what? He'll never make the shot. If you pass your days mumbling, "I'll never make a difference; I'm not worth anything," guess what? You will be sentencing yourself to a life of gloom without parole. Even more, you are disagreeing with God. Questioning his judgment. Second-guessing his taste. According to him you were "skillfully wrought" (Psalm 139:15 NKJV). You were "fearfully and wonderfully made" (v. 14). He can't stop thinking about you! If you could count his thoughts of you, "they would be more in number than the sand" (v. 18).

Why does he love you so much? The same reason the artist loves his paintings or the boat builder loves his vessels. You are his idea. And God has only good ideas.

There's no shortage of voices telling us we aren't quite what we need to be. Our confidence only plummets when we add our own voices to the mix. Refuse to speak doubt, doom, and gloom into your life. Instead, remember this:

My Scripture of Hope

God created human beings in his own image. In the image
of God he created them; male and female he created them.

GENESIS 1:27 NLT

My Anxious Thoughts to Release

God's Promise to Me

I am a handcrafted masterpiece of God's own making.
I was his idea. He calls me wonderful. He will enable
me to do what he has purposed for me to do.

My Prayer

What to Do with Worries

God did not keep back his own Son, but he gave him for us.
If God did this, won't he freely give us everything else?
ROMANS 8:32 CEV

What do we do with our worries? We take our anxieties to the cross—literally. Next time you're worried about your health or house or finances or flights, take a mental trip up the hill. Spend a few moments looking again at the pieces of passion.

Run your thumb over the tip of the spear. Balance a spike in the palm of your hand. Read the wooden sign written in your own language. And as you do, touch the velvet dirt, moist with the blood of God. Blood he bled for you. The spear he took for you. The nails he felt for you. The sign he left for you.

He did all of this for you. Knowing this, knowing all he did for you there, don't you think he'll look out for you here?

God has never promised a life with no storms. But he has promised to be there when we face them.

We worry. We know we're not supposed to. We know that in Christ we have every reason not to worry. But life has storms, and we mess up, and then we ask, *What if . . .* so we worry. What do we do with those worries? Take them to the One who promises to take care of all our worries. If you need a reminder of how willing he is to carry this "worry load" for you, remember this:

My Scripture of Hope

"Do not be afraid or discouraged because of this vast army.
For the battle is not yours, but God's."

2 CHRONICLES 20:15

_____

_____

_____

_____

_____

_____

_____

_____

_____

My Anxious Thoughts to Release

_____

_____

_____

God's Promise to Me

God gave up his own Son for me. Jesus gave up heaven
and died for me. I can trust God to handle my worries.
He will fight through life's storms with and for me.

My Prayer

_____

_____

Jesus' Invitation

*"Take My yoke upon you and learn from Me, for I am gentle
and lowly in heart, and you will find rest for your souls."*
MATTHEW 11:29 NKJV

F armers in ancient Israel used to train an inexperienced ox by yoking it to an experienced one with a wooden harness. The straps around the older animal were tightly drawn. He carried the load. But the yoke around the younger animal was loose. He walked alongside the more mature ox, but his burden was light. In this verse Jesus is saying, "I walk alongside you. We are yoked together. But I pull the weight and carry the burden."

I wonder, how many burdens is Jesus carrying for us that we know nothing about? We're aware of some. He carries our sin. He carries our shame. He carries our eternal debt. But are there others? Has he lifted fears before we felt them? Has he carried our confusion so we wouldn't have to? Those times when we have been surprised by our own sense of peace? Could it be that Jesus has lifted our anxiety onto his shoulders and placed a yoke of kindness on ours?

The kindness of Jesus. We are quick to think of his power, his passion, and his devotion. But those near him know God comes cloaked in kindness. It's a refreshing change from the world that whispers worries, stokes our fears, and feeds our anxieties. It's a change that Jesus invites us to experience anytime and all the time. When you could use a bit of his kindness, remember this:

My Scripture of Hope

"Come to me, all you who are weary and burdened, and I will give you rest."

MATTHEW 11:28

My Anxious Thoughts to Release

God's Promise to Me

I can go to Jesus with my burdens, with my weariness.
I can learn from him. He will soothe me with
gentleness and kindness. He will give me rest.

My Prayer

A Fresh Understanding

He was transfigured before them. His face shone like the
sun, and His clothes became as white as the light.
MATTHEW 17:2 NKJV

How long has it been since a fresh understanding of Christ buckled your knees and emptied your lungs? Since a glimpse of him left you speechless and breathless? If it's been a while, that explains your fears.

When Christ is great, our fears are not. As awe of Jesus expands, fears of life diminish. A big God translates into big courage. A small view of God generates no courage. A limp, puny, fireless Jesus has no power over cancer cells, corruption, identity theft, stock market crashes, or global calamity. A packageable, portable Jesus might fit well in a purse or on a shelf, but he does nothing for your fears.

Don't we need to know the transfigured Christ? One who spits holy fires? Who occupies the loftiest perch and wears the only true crown of the universe, God's beloved Son?

The longer we live in him, the greater he becomes in us. It's not that he changes but that we do; we see more of him. We see dimensions, aspects, and characteristics we never saw before, increasing and astonishing increments of his purity, power, and uniqueness. In the end we fall on our faces and worship. And when we do, the hand of the carpenter touches us. "Arise, and do not be afraid" (Matthew 17:7 NKJV).

Fear is a blindfold. It covers our eyes and blocks our view of our radiant and powerful Savior. How long has it been since the sheer wonder of him left us speechless and breathless? When you need a fresh understanding of him, when you need to tear away the blindfold and feel his touch on your life, remember this:

My Scripture of Hope

It is God who arms me with strength and keeps my way secure.
2 SAMUEL 22:33

_____

_____

_____

_____

My Anxious Thoughts to Release

_____

_____

_____

God's Promise to Me

Our Savior is light, pure and bright. The more I look for him, the more of him I will see. By his power, I can stand. I can carry on.

My Prayer

_____

_____

Never Nearer

He is despised and rejected by men, a Man of
sorrows and acquainted with grief.
ISAIAH 53:3 NKJV

The scene is very simple; you'll recognize it quickly. A grove of twisted olive trees. Ground cluttered with large rocks. A low stone fence. A dark, dark night.

See that solitary figure? Flat on the ground. Face stained with dirt and tears. Fists pounding the hard earth. Eyes wide with a stupor of fear. Hair matted with salty sweat. Is that blood on his forehead?

That's Jesus. Jesus in the Garden of Gethsemane.

We see an agonizing, straining, and struggling Jesus. We see a "man of sorrows." We see a man struggling with fear, wrestling with commitments, and yearning for relief.

We see Jesus in the fog of a broken heart. Jesus is in pain. Jesus is on the stage of fear. Jesus is cloaked, not in sainthood, but in humanity.

Seeing God like this does wonders for our own suffering. God was never more human than at this hour. God was never nearer to us than when he hurt. The Incarnation was never so fulfilled as in the garden.

The next time you are called to suffer, pay attention. Watch closely. It could very well be that the hand that extends itself to lead you out of the fog is a pierced one.

Jesus struggled with fear. Perhaps *struggled* isn't quite the right word. More like *wrestled* or *battled*. When fear has you facedown in the dirt, does it help to know that he's been there before you? That you're not the first to do battle here? When worry limits your view to the dust of the ground, remember this:

My Scripture of Hope

"He will not crush the weakest reed or put out a flickering candle. He will bring justice to all who have been wronged."

ISAIAH 42:3 NLT

_____
_____
_____
_____
_____

My Anxious Thoughts to Release

_____
_____
_____

God's Promise to Me

Jesus understands my sorrows and fears. He's been where I've been. He will help me up and help me stand again.

My Prayer

_____
_____

Worry Stoppers

Let us therefore come boldly to the throne of grace, that we
may obtain mercy and find grace to help in time of need.
HEBREWS 4:16 NKJV

You hate to worry. But what can you do to stop it? These three worry stoppers deserve your consideration:

Pray more. No one can pray and worry at the same time. When we worry, we aren't praying. When we pray, we aren't worrying. "You will keep him in perfect peace, whose mind is stayed on You, because he trusts in You" (Isaiah 26:3 NKJV).

When you pray, you "stay" your mind on Christ, resulting in peace. Bow your knees and banish anxiety.

Want less. Most anxiety stems not from what we need, but from what we want. "Delight yourselves in God, yes, find your joy in him at all times" (Philippians 4:4 PHILLIPS). If God is enough for you, then you'll always have enough, because you'll always have God.

Live for today. Don't sacrifice it on the altar of anxiety. God sends help at the hour we need it.

God meets our daily needs both daily and miraculously.

God sends help at the hour we need it. It's so simple to read and to say. But to believe it when the bills are mounting, the tensions are climbing, and the stack of problems is teetering and ready to fall right on top of you—that's much harder. When you need reassurance that you can, in fact, believe these words, remember this:

My Scripture of Hope

The LORD is my shepherd; I shall not want.

PSALM 23:1 NKJV

_____

_____

_____

_____

_____

_____

_____

_____

My Anxious Thoughts to Release

_____

_____

_____

_____

God's Promise to Me

God is faithful. When I need his wisdom, it will be there.
When I need his strength, it will be there. And when I need
his presence, he will be there. He is enough for me.

My Prayer

_____

_____

God Is Able

"Remember that I am God, and there is no other
God. I am God, and there is no one like me."
ISAIAH 46:9 NCV

N o one breathed life into Yahweh. No one sired him. No one gave birth to him. No one caused him. No act brought him forth.

And since no act brought him forth, no act can take him out. Does he fear an earthquake? Does he tremble at a tornado? Hardly. Yahweh calms the winds with a word. Cancer does not trouble him, and cemeteries do not disturb him. He was here before they came. He'll be here after they are gone. He is uncaused.

And he is ungoverned. Counselors can comfort you in the storm, but you need a God who can still the storm. Friends can hold your hand at your deathbed, but you need a Yahweh who has defeated the grave. Philosophers can debate the meaning of life, but you need a Lord who can declare the meaning of life.

And you need a God who, while so mind-numbingly mighty, can come in the soft of night and touch you with the tenderness of an April snow.

You need a Yahweh. And you have one.

When the worries are big, we need the God who is bigger. When fear chains us, we need the God who breaks the chains. When anxieties steal our breath away, we need the God who is the breath of life. And his promise is that we have him. When you need a reminder that God is not only able but also willing to walk with you through the worries and fears, remember this:

My Scripture of Hope

Ah, Sovereign LORD, you have made the heavens and the earth by your great power and outstretched arm. Nothing is too hard for you.

JEREMIAH 32:17

_____

_____

_____

_____

_____

_____

_____

My Anxious Thoughts to Release

_____

_____

_____

_____

God's Promise to Me

Nothing is impossible for God. He is able to do more than I could ask or imagine. He is the One who walks with me.

My Prayer

_____

_____

Casting Out Fear

We know and rely on the love God has for us. God is love.
Whoever lives in love lives in God, and God in them.

1 JOHN 4:16

Have you ever gone to the grocery on an empty stomach? You're a sitting duck. You buy everything you don't need. Doesn't matter if it is good for you—you just want to fill your tummy. When you're lonely, you do the same in life, pulling stuff off the shelf, not because you need it, but because you are hungry for love.

Why do we do it? Because we fear facing life alone. For fear of not fitting in, we take the drugs. For fear of standing out, we wear the clothes. For fear of appearing small, we go into debt and buy the house. For fear of going unnoticed, we dress to seduce or to impress. For fear of sleeping alone, we sleep with anyone. For fear of not being loved, we search for love in all the wrong places.

But all that changes when we discover God's perfect love. And "perfect love casts out fear" (1 John 4:18 NKJV).

When you know God loves you, you won't be desperate for the love of others. God changes your *n* into a *v*. You go from *lonely* to *lovely*.

> *For the fear*—of facing life alone, of not fitting in, of standing out, of being unseen, of being unloved—what do we do *for the fear*? When you need a reminder that perfect love and a life without fear are just a prayer away, remember this:

My Scripture of Hope

This is how God showed his love to us: He sent his one and only Son into the world so that we could have life through him.

1 JOHN 4:9 NCV

My Anxious Thoughts to Release

God's Promise to Me

God did not create me to live in fear. His Spirit is in me, strengthening me. His perfect love chases away my fears.

My Prayer

DAY 81

Trust God's Goodness

"Why are you fearful, O you of little faith?"
MATTHEW 8:26 NKJV

A great storm arose on the lake so that waves covered the boat, but Jesus was sleeping" (Matthew 8:24 NCV).

Now there's a scene. The disciples scream; Jesus dreams. Thunder roars; Jesus snores. He doesn't doze, catnap, or rest. He slumbers. His snooze troubles the disciples. Matthew and Mark record their responses as three staccato Greek pronouncements and one question.

The pronouncements: "Lord! Save! Dying!" (Matthew 8:25 NKJV).

The question: "Teacher, do You not care that we are perishing?" (Mark 4:38 NKJV).

They do not ask about Jesus' strength: "Can you still the storm?" His knowledge: "Are you aware of the storm?" Or his know-how: "Do you have any experience with storms?" But rather, they raise doubts about Jesus' character: "Do you not care . . ."

Fear does this. Fear corrodes our confidence in God's goodness.

Do the disciples remember the accomplishments of Christ? They may not. Fear creates a form of spiritual amnesia. It dulls our miracle memory. It makes us forget what Jesus has done and how good God is.

Northeasters bear down on the best of us. Contrary winds. Crashing waves. They come. But Jesus still extends his arms. He still sends his angels. Because you belong to him, you can have peace in the midst of the storm.

Storms come. They just do. Sometimes they're huge and sometimes they're simply unrelenting and persistent. They can be storms of

166

circumstances, storms of distress, or storms within our souls. Regardless, the battle is real and we're battered by it. When we need to be reminded of what Jesus has done and how good God is, let's remember this:

My Scripture of Hope

He gives strength to the weary and increases the power of the weak.

ISAIAH 40:29

_____
_____
_____
_____

My Anxious Thoughts to Release

_____
_____
_____

God's Promise to Me

God knows my worries and fears. And he does cares. He cares so much that he chooses to be with me through every storm.

My Prayer

_____
_____

Thirsty Soul

"The water I give will become a spring of water
gushing up inside . . . giving eternal life."
JOHN 4:14 NCV

Deprive your body of necessary fluid, and your body will tell you. Deprive your soul of spiritual water, and your soul will tell you. Dehydrated hearts send desperate messages. Snarling tempers. Waves of worry. Growling mastodons of guilt and fear.

You think God wants you to live with these? Hopelessness. Sleeplessness. Loneliness. Resentment. Irritability. Insecurity. These are warnings. Symptoms of a dryness deep within.

Perhaps you've never seen them as such. You've thought they, like speed bumps, are a necessary part of the journey. Anxiety, you assume, runs in your genes like eye color. Some people have bad ankles; others, high cholesterol or receding hairlines. And you? You fret.

Aren't such emotions inevitable? Absolutely! But unquenchable? No way. View the pains of your heart not as struggles to endure, but as an inner thirst to slake—proof that something within you is starting to shrivel.

Treat your soul as you treat your thirst. Take a gulp. Imbibe moisture. Flood your heart with a good swallow of water.

Where do you find water for the soul? Jesus.

Anxious, fearful thoughts create a thirst deep within us. A thirst for safety, for belonging, for everything to just be all right. We can try to quench that thirst on our own (never lasts), or we can reach out to other people and things (often disastrous). Or we can turn to the only One who offers true relief. When you're thirsty for the living water of Jesus, remember this:

My Scripture of Hope

Jesus declared, "I am the bread of life. Whoever comes to me will never go hungry, and whoever believes in me will never be thirsty."

JOHN 6:35

_____

_____

_____

_____

_____

My Anxious Thoughts to Release

_____

_____

_____

God's Promise to Me

Anxious thoughts do not have to be my constant companion. Jesus will set me free. He will quench my soul's thirst for peace.

My Prayer

_____

_____

No Losing His Love

"My son was dead, but now he is alive again!
He was lost, but now he is found!"

LUKE 15:24 NCV

Jesus summarized God's stubborn love with a parable. He told about a teenager who decided that life at the farm was too slow for his tastes. So with pockets full of inheritance money, he set out to find the big time. What he found instead were hangovers, fair-weather friends, and long unemployment lines. When he'd had just about as much of the pig's life as he could take, he swallowed his pride, dug his hands deep into his empty pockets, and began the long walk home, all the while rehearsing a speech that he planned to give to his father.

He never used it. Just when he got to the top of the hill, his father, who'd been waiting at the gate, saw him. The boy's words of apology were quickly muffled by the father's words of forgiveness. And the boy's weary body fell into his father's opened arms.

No wagging fingers. No clenched fists. No "I told you so!" slaps or "Where have you been?" interrogations. No crossed arms. No black eyes or fat lips. No. Only sweet, open arms. If you ever wonder how God can use you to make a difference in your world, look at the forgiveness found in those open arms and take courage.

We've all been that teenager, even if we were much older than that long-ago prodigal son when we stomped away from God. Our rebellion may last moments, days, or years. We might be in the midst of it right now. Wondering if God will welcome us home can leave us anxious and even avoiding the One we need most. Just remember this:

My Scripture of Hope

See what great love the Father has lavished on us, that we
should be called children of God! And that is what we are!

1 JOHN 3:1

_____

_____

_____

_____

_____

_____

_____

_____

_____

_____

My Anxious Thoughts to Release

_____

_____

_____

God's Promise to Me

God's arms are always open. His mercy is waiting. His grace
is mine. His love does not end. I can fall into him.

My Prayer

_____

_____

A Strong Hand to Hold

O my Strength, I will sing praises to you, for you, O God,
are my fortress, the God who shows me steadfast love.

PSALM 59:17 ESV

With life comes change.

With change comes fear, insecurity, sorrow, stress. So what do you do? Hibernate? Take no risks for fear of failing? Give no love for fear of losing? Some opt to. They hold back.

A better idea is to look up. Set your bearings on the only North Star in the universe—God. For though life changes, he never does.

Consider his strength. Unending.

Daniel calls him "the living God, enduring forever" (Daniel 6:26 ESV). The psalmist tells him, "I will sing of your strength. . . . For you have been to me a fortress and a refuge in the day of my distress" (Psalm 59:16 ESV).

Think about it. God never pauses to eat or asks the angels to cover for him. He never signals a time-out or puts the prayer requests from Russia on hold while he handles South Africa. He "never slumbers or sleeps" (Psalm 121:4 NLT). Need a strong hand to hold? You'll always find one in his.

In the midst of life's big and little changes, sometimes we just need a hand to hold. To comfort, to support, to *not let go*. But not even the best of friends, the best of loves, the best of people can be there for us in every moment of need. Only One can. When you need a reminder that he is holding your hand, remember this:

My Scripture of Hope

"For I am the LORD your God who takes hold of your right
hand and says to you, Do not fear; I will help you."

ISAIAH 41:13

_____
_____
_____
_____
_____
_____
_____
_____
_____
_____

My Anxious Thoughts to Release

_____
_____
_____

God's Promise to Me

God's strength is unending. He is my fortress,
my refuge. His hand holds tight to me.

My Prayer

_____
_____

A Worry-Free Life

*Do not worry about anything, but pray and
ask God for everything you need.*
Philippians 4:6 ncv

Look around you. You have reason to worry. The sun blasts cancer-causing rays. Air vents blow lung-clotting molds. Potato chips have too many carbs. Vegetables, too many toxins. And do they have to call an airport a *terminal*?

Some of us have postgraduate degrees from the University of Anxiety. We go to sleep worried that we won't wake up; we wake up worried that we didn't sleep. We worry that someone will discover that lettuce was fattening all along. The mother of one teenager bemoaned, "My daughter doesn't tell me anything. I'm a nervous wreck." Another mother replied, "My daughter tells me everything. I'm a nervous wreck." Wouldn't you love to stop worrying? Could you use a strong shelter from life's harsh elements?

God offers you just that: the possibility of a worry-free life. Not just less worry, but no worry. "Stay close to me. Talk to me. Pray to me. Breathe me in and exhale your worry." Worry diminishes as we look upward.

Do not worry. Let's be honest. Don't we sometimes look at that verse and think, *Okay, I might as well not breathe*? The world offers us so many reasons to be stressed that worry and its pal anxiety have become a natural part of our days. But they don't have to be. Look up and remember this:

My Scripture of Hope

Depend on the LORD; trust him, and he will take care of you.
PSALM 37:5 NCV

_____

_____

_____

_____

_____

_____

_____

_____

_____

_____

My Anxious Thoughts to Release

_____

_____

_____

God's Promise to Me

I can talk to God. He will listen. And he
will lead me to the peace I need.

My Prayer

_____

_____

His Grace Is Greater

*The more we see our sinfulness, the more
we see God's abounding grace.*
ROMANS 5:20 TLB

To abound is to have a surplus, an abundance, an extravagant portion. Should the fish in the Pacific worry that it will run out of ocean? No. Why? The ocean abounds with water.

Should the Christian worry that the cup of mercy will run empty? He may. For he may not be aware of God's abounding grace. Are you? Are you aware that the cup God gives you overflows with mercy? Are you afraid your mistakes are too great for God's grace?

God is not a miser with his grace. Your cup may be low on cash or clout, but it is overflowing with mercy.

The overflowing cup was a powerful symbol in the days of David. Hosts in the ancient East used it to send a message to the guest. As long as the cup was kept full, the guest knew he was welcome. But when the cup sat empty, the host was hinting that the hour was late. On those occasions, however, when the host really enjoyed the company of the person, he filled the cup to overflowing. He kept pouring until the liquid ran over the edge of the cup and down on the table.[4]

Have you noticed how wet your table is? God wants you to stay.

Of all the things we worry about, there's one worry that is completely unfounded and unnecessary: *Will God really forgive me this time? Does he still want me?* The answer is yes, yes, and forever yes. His grace is always greater. If you are worried about your welcome and hesitant to step into his presence, remember this:

My Scripture of Hope

If we confess our sins, he is faithful and just and will forgive
us our sins and purify us from all unrighteousness.

1 JOHN 1:9

_____

_____

_____

_____

_____

_____

_____

_____

My Anxious Thoughts to Release

_____

_____

_____

God's Promise to Me

God is faithful even when I am not. He has promised
to forgive the sins I confess to him. He will keep
that promise. I am forgiven, and I am his.

My Prayer

_____

_____

A Personal Path

*You, LORD, give perfect peace to those who keep their
purpose firm and put their trust in you.*

ISAIAH 26:3 GNT

When David volunteered to go mano a mano with Goliath, King Saul tried to clothe the shepherd boy with soldier's armor. After all, Goliath stood over nine feet tall. He wore a bronze helmet and a 125-pound coat of mail. He bore bronze leggings and carried a javelin and a spear with a 15-pound head (1 Samuel 17:4–7 NLT). And David? David had a slingshot. This is a VW Bug playing blink with an eighteen-wheeler. When Saul saw David, pimpled, and Goliath, rippled, he did what any Iron Age king would do. "Saul gave David his own armor—a bronze helmet and a coat of mail" (1 Samuel 17:38 NLT).

But David rejected the armor, selected the stones, lobotomized the giant, and taught us a powerful lesson: what fits others might not fit you. Indeed, what fits the king might not fit you. Just because someone gives you advice, a job, or a promotion, you don't have to accept it. Don't be afraid to let your uniqueness define your path of life.

We all, each of us, have a unique path to follow, carved out by God. That's what the Bible tells us. That's what we believe . . . except when we don't. When we see our path as too different, as less than, or not quite what we had in mind. Instead of hiding ourselves away or forcing ourselves into a role God didn't create us to play, remember this:

My Scripture of Hope

The LORD spoke his word to me, saying: "Before I made you
in your mother's womb, I chose you. Before you were born, I
set you apart for a special work."

JEREMIAH 1:4–5 NCV

_____

_____

_____

_____

_____

_____

_____

_____

My Anxious Thoughts to Release

_____

_____

_____

God's Promise to Me

I am God's own creation. I have a unique part to play in
his plan. My best life will be found in following him.

My Prayer

_____

_____

More Like Him

God is kind to you so you will change your hearts and lives.
ROMANS 2:4 NCV

Here's God's agenda for your day: to make you more like Jesus. "God . . . decided from the outset to shape the lives of those who love him along the same lines as the life of his Son" (Romans 8:29 MSG). Do you see what God is doing? Shaping you "along the same lines as the life of his Son."

> Jesus felt no guilt; God wants you to feel no guilt.
>
> Jesus had no bad habits; God wants to do away with yours.
>
> Jesus knew the difference between right and wrong; God wants you to know the same.
>
> Jesus served others and gave his life for the lost; you can do likewise.
>
> Jesus dealt with anxiety about death; you can too.
>
> Jesus faced fears with courage; God wants you to do the same.

Jesus faced his fears with courage. God wants us to do the same. But the question has to be asked: *How? How, Lord?* Isaiah offers the answer. The Lord is the potter, and we are his clay (Isaiah 64:8). But being molded and shaped is not always a comfortable experience. And it takes time. Whether it's worries and fears—or finding the courage to face them—that have you stretched out of shape, trust the One who is shaping you. Remember this:

My Scripture of Hope

I have been crucified with Christ and I no longer live, but Christ lives in me. The life I now live in the body, I live by faith in the Son of God, who loved me and gave himself for me.

GALATIANS 2:20

_____

_____

_____

_____

_____

_____

My Anxious Thoughts to Release

_____

_____

God's Promise to Me

God holds me in his hand. He uses every experience
to make me more like Jesus. I can trust him.

My Prayer

_____

_____

Travel Light

Give all your worries to him, because he cares about you.
1 Peter 5:7 NCV

God has a great race for you to run. Under his care you will go where you've never been and serve in ways you've never dreamed. But you have to drop some stuff. How can you share grace if you are full of guilt? How can you offer comfort if you are disheartened? How can you encourage others when you are anxious? How can you lift someone else's load if your arms are full with your own?

> For the sake of those you love, travel light.
> For the sake of the God you serve, travel light.
> For the sake of your own joy, travel light.

There are certain weights in life you simply cannot carry. Your Lord is asking you to set them down and trust him. He is the father at the baggage claim. When a dad sees his five-year-old son trying to drag the family trunk off the carousel, what does he say? The father will say to his son what God is saying to you.

"Set it down, child. I'll carry that one."

What do you say we take God up on his offer? We just might find ourselves traveling a little lighter.

We carry things. Baggage from the past, worries about the future. We pick them up and forget to put them down. Our arms are full, our minds overloaded, and our bodies riddled with anxiety. We are exhausted and stressed and perhaps more than a little cranky because we're carrying things we were never meant to carry. When you need help unloading, remember this:

My Scripture of Hope

"I will be your God throughout your lifetime—until your hair is white with age. I made you, and I will care for you. I will carry you along and save you."

ISAIAH 46:4 NLT

_____
_____
_____
_____
_____

My Anxious Thoughts to Release

_____
_____
_____

God's Promise to Me

God invites me to give my burdens to him. I can travel light because he carries my burdens—and he carries me.

My Prayer

_____
_____

A Reason to Dance

The LORD is near to all who call upon Him,
to all who call upon Him in truth.
PSALM 145:18 NKJV

God's present is his presence.

God's greatest gift is himself. Sunsets steal our breath. Caribbean blue stills our hearts. Newborn babies stir our tears. Lifelong love bejewels our lives. But take all these away—strip away the sunsets, oceans, cooing babies, and tender hearts—and leave us in the Sahara, and we still have reason to dance in the sand. Why? Because God is with us.

God wants us to know. We are never alone. Ever.

God loves you too much to leave you alone, so he hasn't. He hasn't left you alone with your fears, your worries, your disease, or your death. So kick up your heels for joy.

He is a personal God who loves and heals and helps and intervenes. He looks for reverence, obedience, and God-hungry hearts. And when he sees them, he comes! And when he comes, let the band begin. Let the worries fade. And yes, a reverent heart and a tapping foot can belong to the same person.

We look out at the vastness of the ocean and the endlessness of the night sky, and we wonder, *How could the God who created all that even notice me?* But he does. When we call to him, he promises to guide us from mourning to dancing. When anxiety has you in its grip and you need a reason for joy, remember this:

My Scripture of Hope

You have turned my mourning into joyful dancing. You have
taken away my clothes of mourning and clothed me with joy,
that I might sing praises to you and not be silent.

PSALM 30:11–12 NLT

_____
_____
_____
_____
_____
_____
_____
_____
_____

My Anxious Thoughts to Release

_____
_____
_____

God's Promise to Me

God knows me. _Personally._ His presence is with me. _Personally._
He is bringing to my life reasons for joy. _Personally._

My Prayer

_____
_____

Promise Quick-Reference Guide

DAY 1

ISAIAH 12:2

> **Today's promise:** *The Lord is my light and my salvation. He will lead me out of the prison of fear.*

DAY 2

ISAIAH 41:10

> **Today's promise:** *The Lord is with me. No matter how I feel. No matter what I am facing. The Lord is with me. Always.*

DAY 3

PSALM 139:5 NLT

> **Today's promise:** *I don't have to live afraid. Because God cares. He holds my hands and leads me safely to him.*

DAY 4

PSALM 139:8–10

> **Today's promise:** *I can never go where God is not. He is with me always. And he holds fast to me.*

DAY 5

PSALM 9:10

> **Today's promise:** *Because God is righteous, I can trust his decisions. Because he is sovereign, I can trust his power. I can trust God.*

DAY 6

ROMANS 8:26 NCV

Today's promise: *God hears me always. Even over the noise of life. Even when I don't use words to speak.*

DAY 7

PSALM 18:16

Today's promise: *God is here. He is strong. He has room for me in his eternal lifeboat. He can save me.*

DAY 8

ROMANS 8:31 NKJV

Today's promise: *I can consult Jesus. I can saturate my day in his grace. I can entrust my day to his oversight. I can accept his direction.*

DAY 9

PROVERBS 18:10 NKJV

Today's promise: *I can always turn to God. He will listen to my fears. He will know just what to do. And he will lend me his strength to do it.*

DAY 10

PSALM 37:23–24 NLT

Today's promise: *God knows what I need. He is writing my story. And he will take care of me.*

DAY 11

MATTHEW 17:20–21 NCV

Today's promise: *God moves mountains, so he can remove my worries and make a way through my fears. He will answer my prayers. He will set me free to fly.*

DAY 12

PSALM 25:4–5 NLT

Today's promise: *God sees what I cannot see. He knows the perfect path for me. I can trust him to lead me, step by step, through life's maze.*

DAY 13

ISAIAH 43:1 NCV

Today's promise: *I am not who the world says I am. I am who God says I am. I am his.*

DAY 14

PSALM 32:8 NLT

Today's promise: *God is Lord of all times and places and things. His Word is absolute truth. I can trust and follow him because he knows the way.*

DAY 15

ROMANS 5:8

Today's promise: *With perfect knowledge of all my imperfections, God loves me perfectly. My mistakes do not stun him. His grace still reaches out and saves me.*

DAY 16

ISAIAH 61:10 NLT

Today's promise: *I am sought after by God. His robe of righteousness covers me. His grace erases my guilt. And I can live in his peace.*

DAY 17

PHILIPPIANS 4:19

Today's promise: *God is good. He has promised to provide for me. I can count on him today and tomorrow and every day after that. One day at a time.*

DAY 18

PSALM 23:6 NLT

> **Today's promise:** *I am God's own child. My worries, my fears, my mistakes do not erase his love for me. He will not give up on me.*

DAY 19

2 CORINTHIANS 12:9 NLT

> **Today's promise:** *God lives in me. His power is in me. I never face anything alone. He will work through me and enable me to do what needs to be done.*

DAY 20

JOHN 1:12 NLT

> **Today's promise:** *I don't have to earn my place with God. His grace saves me. He will keep the promises he has made to me. And when I struggle, he will help me believe.*

DAY 21

PSALM 116:1–2 NLT

> **Today's promise:** *God loves to hear from me. I can talk to God anywhere, anytime, about anything. And he will answer me perfectly. Every time.*

DAY 22

2 CORINTHIANS 6:16 NLT

> **Today's promise:** *God is near. He is working in my life. He will carry the weight of this load.*

DAY 23

MATTHEW 7:7–8

> **Today's promise:** *I can pray about anything. I can pray about everything. I can pray any time and all the time. God wants to hear my prayers.*

DAY 24

MATTHEW 10:29–31

Today's promise: *God made me to be me. He will help me be the best I can be. I am both wanted and needed in his world.*

DAY 25

PSALM 46:1

Today's promise: *God's promises do not change. His presence does not change. I'll never face a moment without him to help me.*

DAY 26

ISAIAH 40:11

Today's promise: *God's grace is greater than my guilt. He seeks me and calls me by my name. He won't stop until I am home with him.*

DAY 27

JOHN 16:33

Today's promise: *God will lead me through the challenges of today. He will take care of me tomorrow. His help is always right on time.*

DAY 28

ISAIAH 26:3 NLT

Today's promise: *Because God enjoys perfect power, I can enjoy perfect peace. He stands guard over me.*

DAY 29

ROMANS 8:15 NCV

Today's promise: *God will not reject me. I am his. His love for me is perfect and without end.*

DAY 30

DEUTERONOMY 31:8 NKJV

Today's promise: *Jesus takes my fears seriously. His love and protection cover every detail of my life. I can trust him to watch over me.*

DAY 31

HEBREWS 4:15 NCV

Today's promise: *I can go to Jesus for help. With anything. He will understand. Because he's been where I've been.*

DAY 32

PSALM 8:3–5

Today's promise: *God is infinite and all-powerful. He is also personal. He sees, knows, and loves me.*

DAY 33

EPHESIANS 3:20 NCV

Today's promise: *God is working in my life. He will bless me in surprising ways. And his blessings will be greater than I could ever imagine.*

DAY 34

TITUS 3:4–5 NLT

Today's promise: *God never withholds his kindness from me. He forgives me, loves me, and has a purpose for me.*

DAY 35

JOSHUA 1:9 NLT

Today's promise: *Jesus knows the way because he is the way. I can safely follow him. He will stay with me always.*

DAY 36

JEREMIAH 29:13 NKJV

Today's promise: *God is enough. If I seek him, I will find him. And with him, I will find peace.*

DAY 37

HEBREWS 4:16 NKJV

Today's promise: *The barrier is gone. I am welcome in God's presence any time. And in his presence, I will find peace.*

DAY 38

PSALM 138:8 NLT

Today's promise: *I am God's own work. He created me unlike any other. My unique abilities are part of his design. By using them, I worship and honor him.*

DAY 39

ISAIAH 43:25 NLT

Today's promise: *My mistakes do not lessen God's love. His forgiveness is mine for the asking. He is able to make even my mistakes part of his masterpiece.*

DAY 40

JAMES 1:5 NKJV

Today's promise: *God knows me completely. His love for me is perfect. His friendship is mine forever.*

DAY 41

JEREMIAH 17:7–8

Today's promise: *God's Word is truth. It is active and alive. It comforts me and connects me to Christ.*

DAY 42

PSALM 34:9–10 NCV

> **Today's promise:** *God is generous beyond measure. He has promised to provide for all my needs. He shares his riches and takes care of me.*

DAY 43

ISAIAH 58:11

> **Today's promise:** *I was not made for this place. I belong to God. There is always a place for me with him, at his table, in his family.*

DAY 44

JEREMIAH 29:11

> **Today's promise:** *God loves me simply because I am. I am valuable to him. And he has an amazing destiny planned for me.*

DAY 45

PSALM 62:8

> **Today's promise:** *I can open my heart to Jesus. I can be specific about my fears. He will understand because he has felt all of this too.*

DAY 46

ISAIAH 43:2–3 NCV

> **Today's promise:** *I can expect to see Jesus in my storms. He is with me. He will guide me to peaceful waters.*

DAY 47

ROMANS 8:38–39

> **Today's promise:** *There is no limit to the love of Christ. It stretches beyond infinity. And it surrounds, fills, and embraces me.*

DAY 48

JOHN 3:16

> **Today's promise:** *God does not change. His love does not change. His promises do not change. When I look for him, he will be found. When I need him, he is already there.*

DAY 49

ISAIAH 46:4

> **Today's promise:** *The Lord is the Master of all life's seas. He will keep me from going under. He will get me to the shore.*

DAY 50

JOHN 4:14

> **Today's promise:** *I am invited to drink the living water of Christ's salvation. His Spirit will water, refresh, and revive my soul.*

DAY 51

PSALM 34:4

> **Today's promise:** *God is greater than any giant in my life. Nothing and no one can defeat him. Because he fights for me, I can live free.*

DAY 52

JOHN 10:28–29

> **Today's promise:** *I was bought—redeemed and sealed—by Christ. I belong to him. He protects me with his Spirit who lives in me. This world cannot snatch me away from him.*

DAY 53

2 CORINTHIANS 9:8

> **Today's promise:** *I am a child of God. He put me in this time and place for a purpose. He has filled this time and place with his presence and his provision. With his help, I can see the blessings he has given me.*

DAY 54

PSALM 16:11 NCV

>**Today's promise:** *Each day is God's new creation. It is shining with hope just waiting to be found. He will help me find it.*

DAY 55

1 JOHN 4:4 NCV

>**Today's promise:** *The true I AM is greater than all my worried "I ams." He is with me in this storm. He is the same Savior who defeated the devil. He is here and fighting for me.*

DAY 56

JOHN 17:24

>**Today's promise:** *Jesus has prepared a place for me. He invites me into his presence. He wants me where he is.*

DAY 57

PSALM 62:5–6

>**Today's promise:** *Jesus is the solution to every problem, the answer to every question. He will fill me with all I need.*

DAY 58

JOHN 3:17

>**Today's promise:** *God gives second chances. Each day is a new beginning. And he has filled it with both blessings and plans for me.*

DAY 59

PSALM 18:28

>**Today's promise:** *The Lord is my strength. He will help me take these worrisome thoughts captive. His light will lead me out of the darkness and closer to him.*

DAY 60
PSALM 121:5–8

Today's promise: *God never ceases to watch over me. He guards me, shelters me, defends me. Nothing will touch me that he cannot handle. I am safe in the shadow of his wings.*

DAY 61
LAMENTATIONS 3:22–24 NLT

Today's promise: *The past is covered by God's grace. The future is in his hands. Today is the day I can live—and I can live every moment in his presence.*

DAY 62
JOHN 14:15–17

Today's promise: *The Lord is with me. His Spirit lives in me. I have nothing to fear. Because he who is in me is greater than anything in this world.*

DAY 63
1 PETER 2:9 NCV

Today's promise: *I am chosen. I am a child of God. He called me out of darkness into his light.*

DAY 64
ROMANS 8:28 NKJV

Today's promise: *The Lord is in control. He knows how it all turns out. And he promised it will be for my good. He will give me the courage to keep going and the hope to hold on.*

DAY 65
1 PETER 2:24 NLT

Today's promise: *I am fully and completely known by Jesus. He chose to die for my sins anyway. I cannot lose his love. He will not abandon me.*

DAY 66
PSALM 34:17 NLT

> **Today's promise:** *When I call to God, he will answer. I can entrust my disappointments to him because he cares about me. He will rescue me.*

DAY 67
2 CHRONICLES 16:9 NLT

> **Today's promise:** *God's Spirit within me is greater than any anxiety, any worry, any fear. I can turn to him, and he will strengthen me. He will show me what is real and what is true.*

DAY 68
EPHESIANS 3:18–19 NLT

> **Today's promise:** *The God who made the stars watches over me. He knows my name. He knows all that is coming my way. And he will enable me to do all that truly needs to be done.*

DAY 69
ZEPHANIAH 3:17 NLT

> **Today's promise:** *I am loved. Without end and without conditions. God's love will never fail me.*

DAY 70
ROMANS 8:28

> **Today's promise:** *God is in control. He's working in every detail of my life. He's working it all out for my good. And he's already won.*

DAY 71
PSALM 23:2–3

> **Today's promise:** *God is in perfect control. I can trust him. I can rest in him.*

DAY 72
PHILIPPIANS 4:6–7

Today's promise: *God has already been to the end of this problem. His solution is coming. He will fill me with his peace while I await his answer.*

DAY 73
GENESIS 1:27 NLT

Today's promise: *I am a handcrafted masterpiece of God's own making. I was his idea. He calls me wonderful. He will enable me to do what he has purposed for me to do.*

DAY 74
2 CHRONICLES 20:15

Today's promise: *God gave up his own Son for me. Jesus gave up heaven and died for me. I can trust God to handle my worries. He will fight through life's storms with and for me.*

DAY 75
MATTHEW 11:28

Today's promise: *I can go to Jesus with my burdens, with my weariness. I can learn from him. He will soothe me with gentleness and kindness. He will give me rest.*

DAY 76
2 SAMUEL 22:33

Today's promise: *Our Savior is light, pure and bright. The more I look for him, the more of him I will see. By his power, I can stand. I can carry on.*

DAY 77
ISAIAH 42:3 NLT

Today's promise: *Jesus understands my sorrows and fears. He's been where I've been. He will help me up and help me stand again.*

PSALM 23:1 NKJV

Today's promise: *God is faithful. When I need his wisdom, it will be there. When I need his strength, it will be there. And when I need his presence, he will be there. He is enough for me.*

DAY 79

JEREMIAH 32:17 NIV

Today's promise: *Nothing is impossible for God. He is able to do more than I could ask or imagine. He is the One who walks with me.*

DAY 80

1 JOHN 4:9–10 NCV

Today's promise: *God did not create me to live in fear. His Spirit is in me, strengthening me. His perfect love chases away my fears.*

DAY 81

ISAIAH 40:29

Today's promise: *God knows my worries and fears. And he does cares. He cares so much that he chooses to be with me through every storm.*

DAY 82

JOHN 6:35

Today's promise: *Anxious thoughts do not have to be my constant companion. Jesus will set me free. He will quench my soul's thirst for peace.*

DAY 83

1 JOHN 3:1

Today's promise: *God's arms are always open. His mercy is waiting. His grace is mine. His love does not end. I can fall into him.*

DAY 84

ISAIAH 41:13

Today's promise: *God's strength is unending. He is my fortress, my refuge. His hand holds tight to me.*

DAY 85

PSALM 37:5 NCV

Today's promise: *I can talk to God. He will listen. And he will lead me to the peace I need.*

DAY 86

1 JOHN 1:9

Today's promise: *God is faithful even when I am not. He has promised to forgive the sins I confess to him. He will keep that promise. I am forgiven, and I am his.*

DAY 87

JEREMIAH 1:4–5 NCV

Today's promise: *I am God's own creation. I have a unique part to play in his plan. My best life will be found in following him.*

DAY 88

GALATIANS 2:20

Today's promise: *God holds me in his hand. He uses every experience to make me more like Jesus. I can trust him.*

DAY 89

ISAIAH 46:4 NLT

Today's promise: *God invites me to give my burdens to him. I can travel light because he carries my burdens—and he carries me.*

PSALM 30:11–12 NLT

Today's promise: *God knows me. Personally. His presence is with me. Personally. He is bringing to my life reasons for joy. Personally.*

Notes

1. C. J. Mahaney, "Loving the Church," audiotape of message at Covenant Life Church, Gaithersburg, MD, n.d., quoted in Randy Alcorn, Heaven (Wheaton, IL: Tyndale House, 2004), xxii.

2. Wayne Harris-Wyrick, "More Stars Than Grains of Sand on Earth? You Bet," *The Oklahoman*, February 4, 2019, https://www.oklahoman.com/story/lifestyle/2019/02/05/more-stars-than-grains-of-sand-on-earth-you-bet/60474645007/.

3. Monica Young, "How Big Is Betelgeuse Really?" *Sky & Telescope*, November 6, 2020, https://skyandtelescope.org/astronomy-news/how-big-is-betelgeuse-really/.

4. From a sermon entitled "God's Antidote to Your Hurt" by Rick Warren.

About the Author

S ince entering the ministry in 1978, Max Lucado has served churches in Miami, Florida; Rio de Janeiro, Brazil; and San Antonio, Texas. He currently serves as Teaching Minister of Oak Hills Church in San Antonio. He is the recipient of the 2021 ECPA Pinnacle Award for his outstanding contribution to the publishing industry and society at large. He is America's bestselling inspirational author with more than 145 million products in print.

Visit his website at MaxLucado.com
Facebook.com/MaxLucado
Instagram.com/MaxLucado
Twitter.com/MaxLucado
Youtube.com/MaxLucadoOfficial
The Max Lucado Encouraging Word Podcast